THE LEGACY OF HERMANN COHEN

Program in Judaic Studies
Brown University
BROWN JUDAIC STUDIES
Edited by
Jacob Neusner,
Wendell S. Dietrich, Ernest S. Frerichs, William Scott Green,
Calvin Goldscheider, David Hirsch, Alan Zuckerman

Project Editors (Project)

David Blumenthal, Emory University (Approaches to Medieval Judaism)
William Brinner (Approaches to Judaism and Islam)
Ernest S. Frerichs, Brown University (Dissertations and Monographs)
Lenn Evan Goodman, University of Hawaii (Studies in Medieval Judaism)
William Scott Green, University of Rochester (Approaches to Ancient Judaism)
Norbert Samuelson, Temple University (Jewish Philosophy)
Jonathan Z. Smith, University of Chicago (Studia Philonica)

Number 167
THE LEGACY OF HERMANN COHEN

by
William Kluback

THE LEGACY OF HERMANN COHEN

by
Willliam Kluback

Scholars Press
Atlanta, Georgia

THE LEGACY OF HERMANN COHEN

Copyright © 1989 by Brown University
Paperback edition published 2010 by Brown Judaic Studies

All rights reserved. No part of this work may be reproduced or transmitted in any form or by any means, electronic or mechanical, including photocopying and recording, or by means of any information storage or retrieval system, except as may be expressly permitted by the 1976 Copyright Act or in writing from Brown Judaic Studies, Brown University, Box 1826, Providence, RI 02912.

Library of Congress Cataloging-in-Publication Data

Kluback, William.
   The Legacy of Hermann Cohen / by William Kluback.
     p. cm. — (Brown Judaic studies ; 167)
   Bibliography : p.
   ISBN 1-55540-322-0 (alk. paper)—ISBN 978-1-930675-76-6 (paper: alk. paper)
   I. Cohen, Hermann. 1842–1918. II. Title
B3216.C74K657   1989
193—dc 19   89-4148
                                  CIP

Printed in the United States of America
on acid-free paper

Dedicated to My Friends
Israel Glasser
Manfred Riedel

Contents

	Preface: An Endeavor to Begin	*ix*
1	The Ecumenical Meaning of Cohen's *Religion of Reason*	*1*
2	Monotheism and History: The Heritage of Hermann Cohen	*17*
3	Time and History: The Conflict between Hermann Cohen and Franz Rosenzweig	*43*
4	The Conflict with Myth and Evil	*57*
5	The Despair of Ressentiment and the Power of Compassion	*73*
6	The Abyss of Contradiction: Peace and Hatred	*93*
7	The Opposition to Kantian Ethics	*107*
8	The Aesthetic Consciousness and the *Religion of Reason*	*125*
9	Hermann Cohen and W. A. Mozart	*139*
	Conclusion	*163*
	Notes	*165*

Preface:
An Endeavor to Begin

In an article originally written to celebrate the fiftieth anniversary of Hermann Cohen's death, Karl Löwith made the following remark:

> Cohen's philosophical error was not his struggle to know himself as a German Jew, but that he believed it necessary to have Germany as a homeland, *vaterländischen Heimat;* to believe that as a philosopher it was necessary to have a homeland, as if the historical age and environment in which we are accidentally born is the one undivided world for which philosophy as the thought of this oneness is concerned.[1]

Löwith's words refer and question the essence of philosophy, and Cohen's in particular. In many ways philosophy is inseparable from the situation in which it is born, and the needs to which it responds. The social and political problems of the society in which it functions make demands upon it, and philosophy must respond to them. Cohen never allowed himself to be divorced from the struggles for individual dignity and social responsibility. The constant fight against anti-Semitism, social injustice, cultural pessimism could never be avoided or denied. Perhaps there is a philosophy, a love of the truth which is universal and timeless, but it is so only because we are here and now. Yes, we can say that Cohen lost the battle; in 1942 his wife Martha was deported to Theresienstadt. Cohen loved a Germany which never existed or could never be; but we know that after the fact.

To believe is efficacious; to refuse to affirm a purpose, to surrender to indifference and arbitrariness, is to return to violence. Cohen would say that "for my own peace I need the confidence that hatred among peoples will be destroyed from the consciousness of mankind."[2] Naïve, the worldly wise among us will say; man is "nasty, brutish and short." Kant understood Hobbes well. Couldn't Cohen foresee Hitler and Martha's death? Cohen was a philosopher, not a sage. The sage does not need to believe; he knows. What is remarkable is that the philosopher is committed to reason in defiance of violence and that he affirms the universal discourse of reason when circumstances deny it, and when his belief makes him a fool for his fellow man.

The study of the work of Hermann Cohen should not be limited to questions of his Kant interpretation. In fact, we would say that it requires a knowledge of German politics and cultural movements in the nineteenth and early twentieth centuries. Cohen's work belongs not only to the history of philosophy, but to European civilization. The struggle to hold forth the moral law as the embodiment of the ideal of humanity in a civilization still rooted in atavism and racism could, with veracity, be considered a fool's endeavor. What is so astounding is the courage and commitment which Cohen developed throughout his life. We would agree with Löwith, who said that "the philoso-pher Cohen was always a Jewish theologian, and even became more so."[3] The idea of God belonged to the origin and distinction of a people. It had creative power, the force to mold and structure, to give life and perpetuate it, to be a demand and a command, to separate what *is* from what *should be*. "Monotheism is not the thought of one man, but of the whole Jewish national spirit unfolding in the cration and development of this thought which impregnates the entire thinking of the people."[4] The depth of Cohen's understanding of man can be measured by his conviction that man can become a different being if a new world were placed before him. The new world is the ethical, the struggle for universality, the eternal task and responsibility of philosophy. To comprehend Cohen we must grasp a philosopher whose belief could never be separated from his thought and actions, and who knew that such separation was possible but sterile. The more devoted he was to philosophy, the more devoted he was to God. The strength which he drew from his God became the strength which he gave to reason. His life was the "great refusal" to pantheism, to the reduction of ethics to logic. He lived the prophetic denial of imagery. No image could embody divinity, i.e., no philosophical system should end that primordial division between what *is* and what *should be*. No artistic beauty can capture divinity, no object is adequate. The struggle against idolatry does not belong only to the religious; it is reason's perennial endeavor to free reality from myth and the demonic attachment to the given. This is the source and force of Cohen's Idealism.

The various chapters in this volume attempt to explore the multiple aspects and implications of Cohen's philosophy. His last and most endearing work represents a grand synthesis of reason and belief. The heritage which flows from it continues that never-ending conflict between the particular and the "breakthrough to universality." The primacy of the ethical linked Cohen to Kant. It made it possible for him to acknowledge that moral dualism between being, *Sein,* and existence, *Dasein.* "The share of reason in monotheism is strongly confirmed in this distinction (being and existence). For existence is attested by the senses, through perception. On the other hand, it is reason which, against all sense-appearance, bestows actuality upon existence, discovers and elevates the nonsensable [*sic*] to being, and marks it out as true being."[5] There can be no uniting of being and existence without the idolatry of the particular. Indeed, it is this idolatry which denies the freedom of the moral subject, which suffocates that primordial negation that is the essence of freedom. Cohen's philosophy was the grand refusal to the dominance of existent. His was the belief in the idea, the vision of the future, the belief in the ever-renewed creation for which each man has a shared responsibility. "Thus what the study of nature and of man has sufficiently shown elsewhere may well be true here, viz., that the inscrutable wisdom through which we exist is not less worthy of venerating in respect to what it denies us than in what it has granted."[6] The battle against idolatry creates the forces of Idealism. What need would there be for Idealism if there were no idolatry?

We will show how deeply rooted is Socialism in Cohen's thought. No better illustration of this attitude and commitment than the remark made about Job in Kants *Begründung der Ethik:* "The Job of our age asks no longer whether man has more sunshine than rain, and whether in the distributing justification of pleasure there is a calculated order: an increase in the pleasure of one in the realm of morality necessitating a decrease for the other."[7] Through all Cohen's writing, the social consequences of reason in every realm of expression are clearly demonstrated. No philosopher paid closer attention to moral and political problems than did Cohen. Cohen, who loved so dearly the idea of Humanity, knew that love was not enough, that man was a doer; he neede to make decisions, and these carried responsibilities. In situation, the realization of the ethical begins. Cohen rejected any theory of evil which would lessen human responsibility. Clearly and precisely he refused to comprehend Kant's notion of radical evil as anything more than a temporal aberration. Quoting Kant, he stated: "The principle of inborn evil is immoral thought of no value."[8] Whatever man's distructive inclinations be, they can be changed. Man can renounce his previous ways of living.

This was Cohen's commitment to the unending moral task of philosophy. Could a philosophy of religion be possible without such a belief? Could a universal discourse of reason make sense without the possibility to overcome violence, the possibility of which is freedom? Cassirer told us the obvious truth when he stated that National Socialism wanted to break the control which the Jews of Germany had on political and cultural life, revealing that unrequited love of German literature, that love of the *Humanitätsideal* which Cohen unhappily identified with the German. It was indeed an unrequited love, now so real to us through the commentaries of G. Scholem, R. Minder, and L. Löwith. Yet, the influence of Cohen is profound. If it were refused by Hartmann and Heidegger and their followers, it has its success in Eric Weil. It is difficult to read Weil's *Logique de la philosophie,* his moral and political philosophy, without being deeply impressed by his stress on the reasonable, on the universal discourse of philosophy, on the need for a "breakthrough to the universal." I don't mean to say that Weil is a Cohenian; I only say that his devotion to the universal, his fear of the demonic particular, his emphasis on action, meaning, and moral consciousness indicate that this student of Cassirer remained loyal to Cohen. The loyalty is to reason, to the primacy of the ethical. This is Cohen's heritage. This heritage is built on the Prophets of Israel, Plato, Leibniz, Kant. We could say that it lives wherever man is committed to reason, to the moral law, and to God as the principle of truth.

1

The Ecumenical Meaning of Cohen's *Religion of Reason*

Rarely was the philosopher Hermann Cohen so personal in his expression as when he declared in the last chapter of his book *Religion of Reason out of the Sources of Judaism* (1919):

> For my own peace I need the confidence that hatred among people will be destroyed from the consciousness of mankind. People do not have to hate one another, but greed awakens envy, and greed and envy delude man with an illusory image, which one passes off as a power of the soul, and which one presumes to confirm as such. All hatred is vain and wanton.[1]

I was always struck by the pathos of this remark. It seemed to touch the depths of the inner moral universe of Cohen's commitment to the reality of the future, to that deepest of beliefs that philosophy is ultimately a willingness to take one's stand in the moral universe knowing that its being or nonbeing is dependent upon the commitment I make, and the belief I am willing to defend even to death. The reading of Cohen's great works, in Ethics, Logic, Aesthetics, and Religion cannot but impress those who seek meaning in history and those who know that moral decision and action are the ground of the philosophical experience. Cohen was a guardian of the religious and philosophical heritage which never wavered in its belief that man had the capacity to decide between the good and the bad, that intention and responsibility were the vital elements of moral life and that hope and optimism could never be separated from the confidence we have in the power of mankind to overcome adversity, pain, and pessimism.

> As long as hatred threatens me, my own or another man's, I cannot hope for peace and for genuine contentment. If the misery of war did not rage about us, then even the specter of war, the mere danger of war, would constitute a contradiction to the peace of the world, as well as to the peace of the soul. . . . Nor can the individual man attain peace of soul without securing the peace of the world.[2]

The last sentence reveals a moral universalism which necessarily belongs to the philosophical spirit. The universal and the individual are intimately tied to each other not only logically but morally. Cohen spoke as the philosopher of Humanity; he made words like *justice, truthfulness,* and *courage* have both theoretical and practical meaning. He spoke like a prophet, convinced and dedicated to the fact that there is moral responsibility attached to those who undertake to speak to their fellow men. The philosopher above all must keep before mankind the hope and belief in the future betterment of human relationship and understanding. Man's need to inquire about the purpose of history is fundamental for those who are given to thinking. Cohen knew that he had the responsibility to formulate a philosophical and theological expression of history. He turned to both the religious and philosophical tradition to find the possibility of a structure in and through which mankind as an idea could become a reality. Cohen finished his great text on the religion of reason at the end of World War I. His reflections on war, hatred, envy, and greed were fed by the pain of the world in which he lived. The philosopher lives in his world and imbibes its sufferings. He lives with the inadequacies and prejudices of his fellow men; in all the greed and ambition which he sees about him he builds his hope and joy in the future, his idea of Mankind, the strength of his belief in the "new heavens and new earth."

Karl Löwith was a philosopher who gave serious attention to the philosophy of history. Driven from his homeland, he lived in both East and West. He thought about history in his essays *Gesammelte Abhandlungen, Zur Kritik der geschichtlichen Existenz,* in books on Jacob Burckhardt, in studies on Hegel, Nietzsche, and Valéry; and in his much-cited volume *Meaning in History*. It is these reflections which I believe have significant meaning for our comprehension of history, philosophy, and theology. In many ways they relate to each other. In the very first pages of his book *Meaning in History* Löwith cites Cohen: "The concept of history is a product of prophetism."[3] The references to Cohen's *Religion of Reason* are rare, and individual citation causes great interest, which is heightened when we read Löwith's conclusions:

> The very calamities of their national history strengthened and enlarged the prophetic faith in the sovereignty of the divine purpose; for He who sets empires in motion for judgment could use them for deliverance as well. The possibility of a belief in the providential ordering of world-historical destinies depends on this belief in a holy people of universal significance, because only peoples, not individuals, are a proper subject of history and only a holy people is directly related to the Lord as Lord of history. Christians are not a historical people.[4]

In fact, Löwith goes on to say that "only the Jews are really historical people, constituted as such by religion, by the act of the Sinaitic revelation."[5] We are faced with two realities; the one which is Christian is "the story of salvation as embodied in Jesus Christ," who "redeems and dismantles as it were the hapless history of the world." On the other hand, "one has to conclude that a Jewish theology of secular history is indeed a possibility and even a necessity, while a Christian philosophy of history is an artificial compound."[6] Our concern is not so much the contrast as it is to understand from Cohen's *Religion of Reason* the validity of Löwith's judgment. If, as I believe, Cohen's work is the fundamental text of contemporary Jewish thought, from which and to which any serious attempt to grasp the philosophy of religion must and should begin, then an exploration of Cohen's ideas concerned with history, future, people, must not only be seriously investigated, but their universal implications developed.

Cohen had his particular "enemies," and they included cultural pessimism, mythology, pantheism, historical determinism. Monotheism spoke of the incomparable and unique nature of God, whose relationship with man becomes moral task and responsibility. The love which man has for God becomes the responsibility to struggle for the uniqueness of the idea in a world yet unable and unwilling to receive the idea. The incomparable nature of God makes it impossible to identify Him with any person, event, or thing. God is infinite task; the infinity which lies in thinking, doing, and feeling. Purity is the only adjective which is proper for logic, ethics, and aesthetics because they must proceed from autonomy. Idealism as the embodiment of this purity is ultimately and essentially the philosophical expression of Monotheism. Idealism and Monotheism are one. What has made it so difficult to comprehend Cohen's philosophical system has been the failure to identify the purity of the monotheistic God with the purity, i.e., autonomy, of the philosophic spirit in thinking, doing, and feeling. Cohen remains incomprehensible without a radical grasp of God's incomparable and distinct nature, which defies and refuses identification, analogy, and comparison with what exists or with what we call real. This denial of comparison makes it possible to refuse reality to what is given, to demand that the what is, must and should become what it can yet be. Nothing in the given is to be allowed fixity or permanency. Everything that *is* is *yet-to-be*. The future is the meaning of Monotheism as the future becomes the infinitesimal in thinking, doing, and feeling. World history is at its beginning. Monotheism is not at the beginning, but at the end. World history is moved by the love of this idea. "Mankind did not live in any past and did not become alive in the present; only the future can bring about its bright and beautiful form. The form is an idea, not a shadowy image of the beyond."[7] If forced to be historically determined we become cultural pessimists and historical materialists. No dangers could be more serious than the loss of the future as the supreme category of time. In historical pessimism man seeks salvation through the violent, the distorted, and the romantic. Racism, national antagonisms, and ideological fantasies of holy blood and soil become the vision of liberation. They are the ever-renewed myths into which man escapes if he needs salvation from historical and moral pessimism.

Cohen makes a clear contrast between the myth of Zagraeus and the stories of the Flood. Their concreteness makes illustration possible and sensible. Zagraeus is the dismembered god whose limbs are scattered throughout the world and, at the same time, seek to be reunited with each other. We are witness to a divine life: dismemberment and reunification, the dying and rebirth of divinity. This life is not only in the god, but in nature and in man. Here we have discovered a key which unlocks not only divine, but human and natural life. The process is continually repeated. No change, no interruption, but an ongoing dismemberment and renewal. Each reality must die and be reborn, must be separated and rejoined, must endure confusion to find order. "Nowhere, however, does mythical thought achieve in this respect more lucidity or clearness of penetration. Everything in the myth remains history, in the sense of the past; never and nowhere does history appear as the idea of the future of mankind under the guidance of God."[8] The repetition of the past ends the need for ethics. Man must imitate, must become like the god, participate in his death and birth, in the pain of his dismemberment and the joy of his redemption. God is life and personality, His meaning is not the yet-to-be. Nothing threatened religion and ethics more deeply than the implications of mythical thinking. Cohen's eyes were always upon the future. The being or the nonbeing of moral world were at stake for Him in how we conceived time and God.

With a radical sense of difference Cohen deals with the meaning of the Flood. The story illustrates the purity of monotheism; it embodies a covenant between God and Noah, "this fact in itself is important." The significance of *this* covenant is unique because it is one with mankind. "And what is the content of this covenant? Nothing else, nothing less than the *preservation,* thus the future, of the human race."[9] The fact that there is a covenant between man and God, between God and nature, forces us to see the bond between heaven and earth, to know there is a symbol, the *rainbow,* which points to the infinite development of mankind and the assurance that this development will not be destroyed. Here begins that correlation between man and God, that tie with earth, with man's responsibility for its preservation and fructification. Never is the earthly to be disparaged, never is there to be a radical separation between spirit and matter. The history of mankind belongs to a covenant which embraces creation in all its multiple aspects. Toward creation there is no holy and no profane division. The holy and profane are the judgments upon man's attitude and treatment of what has been lent to him by the divine. Noah's covenant refuses any duality; the goodness of creation depends upon man's realization of its purpose; man's distortions only cause it to pour forth the pollution which man forces upon it. Man cannot be satisfied with what is. He can never allow himself to identify the real and the reasonable. If the ideal is always in the distant future and is not a fixed reality but an ethical task, if we are always required to relate what *is* to what *can be,* and the what can be to the ideal, then we can speak of human life as dwelling in the comparative. Refusing to be captured by the given, unable to impose the ideal we live in the comparative. We do not destroy reality by opposing it to the superlative; we advance reality by working for the better. It is through the efforts of the better that we stand within the realities of moral life. The best is yet to be; the given is what must always be improved; the better depends upon human moral decision, action, and prudence. It is the mediation between the divine and the natural. In it the consciousness of moral existence finds its efficacy in moral action. Action is always in the mediating realm acting upon the positive, softening the demands of the superlative, and giving to human life the humaneness which it needs and requires to sharpen man's sensitivities and strengthen his human feeling. The covenant between God and mankind requires the life of a people whose experiences drive them forward, but, at times, also sideways and even backwards. Historical existence embraces the body as well as the soul, the compromise of conditions and a level of moral and religious awareness, but it is here in the inadequacy and incompleteness of the moral and political that we confront with intensity the responsibility for God's covenant and the demands of His incomparable essence.

"If we understand," says Karl Löwith, "as we must, Christianity in the sense of the New Testament and history in our modern sense, i.e., as a continuous process of human action and secular development, a 'Christian history' is nonsense.... The world after Christ has assimilated the Christian perspective toward a goal and fulfillment and, at the same time, has discarded the living faith in an imminent *eschaton.*"[10] Cohen had a different perspective. Religion and ethics are inseparable. The meaning of human existence depends upon the moral deed whose comprehension belongs to logic and whose developed sense of feeling belongs to aesthetics. What this all means is that the divine-human relationship becomes a corelationship which preserves man's nature and integrity. The possibility of an *imminent eschaton* is excluded from Cohen's perspective. Man and people bear the responsibility for the realization of nature and spirit in and through the history of the world. The divine in no way diminishes man's central position as the embodiment of moral self-consciousness. History is judged by the covenant at each stage of its development and consciousness. "In this one covenant of all mankind the Kingdom of God is realized on earth. God's covenant with Noah is completed in this covenant of God with mankind. The covenant of mankind, as the unification of all men is the covenant of man with God. The covenant is the sign, the guarantee, of God's government of the world."[11] Faced as we are with the constant question about the meaning of human existence, it would seem that it is this question which Cohen faced throughout his life. In fact, we could say that he philosophized from the conviction and belief that life had meaning because God is, and we might ask ourselves if there is any other way to think. Philosophers from antiquity on began with what we call the faith of reason. Cohen's conviction that Monotheism and Idealism were one rested upon the assumption that God as the principle of truth was inseparable from that of reason as the purity of knowledge. The corelationship between man and God preserved the distinction between them. Relationship preserves distinction and distinction is the guarantor of relationship. Whatever be God's omnipotence, man never loses the capacity to think, to act, and to feel in such a way that he lends dignity to the reason he didn't create, but which he continuously discovers. This discovery is the eternal history of that unique corelationship between man as reason and God as the principle of truth.

> The government of the world, as the setting of an end for the world, and the realization of it, in the world, is the meaning and content of monotheism.... The government of the world is the moral order of the world. If morality and nature are different methodologically, then the order of the world, as moral order, must be the government of the world, and this establishes the difference between monotheism and pantheism.[12]

Intimately tied to the idea of a moral order distinct from the order of nature is the requirement of Judgment. Judgment becomes a "remembrance" of the covenant. The past is recalled in order that the future be clear; the present is comprehended with the meaning of the future. The covenant binds together the Judgment and the Judged. The moral universe and the idea of Humanity are formed in this tie between the Judgment and the Judged. We could speak of God's love as God's Judgment and of man's love as the love of the Judged for the obligation and need which is embraced in the Judgment of love. Love entails responsibility, it demands knowledge; it refuses the romantic embracements which overwhelm the intellect into the sensuous. "Ethics defines its God to itself as the guarantor of morality on earth, but beyond the definition, beyond postulating this idea, its means fall. The peculiar contribution of religion to the ethical idea of God is the trust in God, the confidence in the messianic fulfillment of the idea."[13] Important for Cohen is that both ethics and religion make contributions to the idea of God. It is vain to attempt to weigh the importance of the contribution that each makes to this supreme idea. In fact, we could say that without the ethical the religious becomes impossible, but we could also add that Cohen's conception of Idealism already presupposed the idea of God. Trust in God doesn't suddenly arise from a mistrust in reason or feeling; it is prepared for in them. The very act of thinking on a serious level is trust in logic. The need to act, the realization that the moral order depends upon action, is an act of trust. I believe that Cohen's system and his thoughts on the religious necessitate each other. He was religious in philosophy and philosophical in his faith. Could we not equally say that the theologian lives in the philosopher and the philosopher in the theologian? I find it difficult to draw them so far apart that they belong to different universes. Discussing prayer and thinking, Cohen inserts these remarks: "all thinking of this language [prayer] about God and about man, all the thinking of this correlation, would remain theoretical if prayer were not that activity of language in which the will becomes active in all the means of thought."[14] It might, at first, seem quaint that Cohen would infuse the language of prayer into the theoretical expressions about corelationship; yet we are aware that theoretical language is not always adequate to express the faith that lies behind the commitment to ideas, and we search for more fulfilling forms in metaphors and symbols to reveal realities which theory hides, or at the most, veils.

Cohen doesn't often speak of the symbol, but at the end of his discussion of law he makes pertinent remarks about its efficacy:

> The symbol, on the other hand, extends beyond the special image of its own representation and reaches out to the infinity of images and forms which it evokes and therefore brings forth. As great as the danger of symbol is, as great is its encompassing value. If we consider the law as a symbol, we exceed the expression with which the Mishnah distinguishes the law from

the teaching, calling the law the 'fence around the teaching.' The law is not only a fence which isolates the teaching in order to guard and protect it, but considered as a symbol, it becomes a lever which is not only a positive support of the teaching, but a means for engendering the teaching.[15]

The value of this long quotation is to show that symbolic thinking becomes the essential mode of revelation when we are dealing with the search for meaning, and we know that meaning cannot be fixed and determined like myth, but that it is a continuous process of development and growth. "Symbolic imagination and intelligence," to use an expression of Cohen's student Ernst Cassirer, is the distinguishing characteristic of man, and when this power of imagination is linked to the will and to trust in God's covenant, then we have the sources from which symbols and metaphors emerge, elucidate, and extend what theoretical language can only analyze and put forth in systematic order. The introduction of symbolic interpretation makes it possible to comprehend Cohen's *Religion of Reason* with multiple possibilities and from perspectives not previously indicated.

If we interpret a particular history religiously, then we must be able to comprehend that history as a transfiguration of secular reality into ethical universalism. Cohen was deeply concerned with this transfiguration and devoted several chapters of the *Religion of Reason* to the question of virtues. Cohen says that "without this self-transformation of the chosen people into messianic mankind Jewish truthfulness could hardly have been maintained. From the very beginning, however, the logical power of the truth of the unique God continuously held open the perspective of a messianic mankind."[16] The question of truthfulness immediately dawns upon us. Cohen never yielded to attempts to give religion an autonomy which would allow it the right to rival ethics and even stand in contradiction to ethics. What many have thought a weakness—Cohen's inability to free himself from philosophical rationalism—I believe is his greatest victory. "Religion has its peculiarity, but in no way does it have autonomy with regard to ethics."[17] Nothing must violate the purity of moral self-consciousness. The pure will, like pure thinking, makes it possible to conceive of God as holiness. We cannot grasp God in any way but as the "archetype of human morality." Every attribute which flows from this holiness becomes an expression of His truth. "God's holiness is identical with God's uniqueness." The virtues are the ways to morality. From the human point of view God is the moral task placed upon man to achieve the ways of virtue; they are the critique of empirical reality. God as truth obliges man to truthfulness. "Religious truthfulness also guards against false determination of the relationship between religion and philosophy. The thesis 'credo quia absurdum' becomes entirely impossible. Equally the separation between faith and reason is only permissible for the purpose of methodological distinction."[18] God's truth is inseparable from His moral legislation. For a historical people nothing is more significant than the Law. God's holiness is embraced only in God's law. No separation can be made between the divine essence and its moral and juridical consequences. A people who live with their God and who have formed a covenant with Him need law. They are as a people, a society, but, like no other society, they are committed to the Law of God. Whatever they say of God they transform into moral and civil legislation. The truth of God requires the truthfulness of man. It permits no doctrine of the absurd, no radical differentiation between faith and reason. That God is truth demands a comprehension of this truth in and through the truthfulness of man's actions in his relationships with his fellow men and in his relationship to himself. "Truthfulness is an absolute virtue. It can never be violated. Nevertheless, it puts on man demands that seem to exceed the measure of man."[19] Truthfulness must be balanced with modesty. Knowing that man's moral nature and existence make it impossible for him to be consistently truthful, modesty accounts for man's weakness and inadequacy. It refuses to allow exceptions to truthfulness in theory, but in practice modesty is the source of man's awareness of his fallible nature and the distorted possibilities of existence. Man's humble and modest comprehension of his inadequacies and dependencies becomes the living sources of his experience and knowledge of the absolute nature and demand of truthfulness. My purpose is not to analyze the virtues but to indicate that God's relationship to a historical people is more than that to a community of saints. It is a relationship to sin-prone beings. Here we deal with political, economic, and social life embodying all the weaknesses and inadequacies of societal life. This is not a community embracing eternity, but one confronting national and international relationships, domestic and national politics. In all these affairs man's animal qualities are as prevalent as his dignified behavior. What is different is the awareness of God's presence and his covenant with the generations who are not only present but who are yet to come. If man is required to be humble before his God, he is necessitated to be modest before his fellow man. "Human consciousness is surrounded by so many ensnaring dangers of self-esteem that it would not be able to assert and preserve its modesty if the latter were not directed by humility before God. Before God, all men are equal."[20] To believe in the possibility of a "holy people," to have hope in the future as the supreme moment of time, to reject inherited guilt and the sufferings of punishment and the dualism between the "saved" and the "damned," means that we have placed ethics at the center of philosophical thinking. The being or nonbeing of the world is a moral question whose answer cannot be given in myths and theogonies, but only where God as the principle of truth is the demand for truthfulness in man, in other words, where the being of God is the consequent moral responsibility of man and the "holy people" a symbol for that community to the idea of Humanity.

Cohen was deeply influenced by the symbol of God's suffering servant found in the fifty-third chapter of Isaiah: "The 53rd Chapter of Isaiah is perhaps the greatest wonder of the Old Testament."[21] If we ask why this picture of the suffering servant was so meaningful for Cohen, we are faced with both a philosophical and religious problem. Cohen, who perceived of the virtues as ways to the moral life, was convinced that courage was the source and strength of philosophical and religious life. "Courage is the triumph of humanity, just as justice coupled with love is the embodiment of God's attributes."[22] Man's courage flows from his conception of God as the doer of mighty deeds. Cohen was aware that the philosopher of Idealism must have the courage to set forth ideas which were not easily comprehensible and acceptable to his fellow men. The struggle for ideas was inseparable from the one which Cohen fought with those who perpetuated racism, national hatreds, and romantic marriages with mythical pasts. The meaningfulness of such ideas as Humanity and God had to come up against political and social atavism, racism, which were entrenched in prejudice and strengthened by intellect and cowardice. But the struggle of Idealism had to be continued within philosophy itself where cultural pessimism, anarchistic individualism, and the undermining of reason became part of that same philosophical discourse. Cohen identified himself with man's need for meaning, for reasonable discourse and a concept of history that embodied the feeling for mankind and a sensitivity for humaneness.

He believed that it was "an unparalleled irony of history that the story of Jesus Christ's life, sealed by his death, should have become the main difference between Christianity and Judaism."[23] Isaiah's suffering servant was Cohen's symbol of those who suffered for ideas and for justice, i.e., social and economic justice among men. The "remnant of Israel," a poetic symbol which embraced what he called in traditional language the "sufferings of love." Not suffering tied to sin, but the consequence of free moral choice. If Christ meant anything to Cohen it was his intimate connection to this "remnant of Israel." This remnant is the moral history of mankind. Here the future was embraced in hope. Hope is not a fiction of the imagination but an integral moment of moral self-consciousness. Bearing within itself consequences not always conducive to happiness, it manifested the commitment to morality, to the monotheistic view of a humanity which transcended national borders and racial divisions. If the figure of Christ divided Judaism from Christianity, then Cohen hoped that future generations would see in this separation a falsity. How could the suffering Jesus, the teacher of parables, living in the light of Isaiah, become the source of conflict and hatred? "The philosophy of history of future generations will have to consider and fathom this riddle of the most intimate history of the spirit, as far as it has unfolded up to this time."[24] The philosophy of history is one with the discourse of reason, the refusal to deny that the world has meaning and purpose and that man's life when committed to thinking and acting is the source and continuity of this discourse. Cohen found it necessary to comprehend the tradition in which he was born and to which he remained devoted throughout his life. Deep within the philosophical structures which he elaborated in his System was his need to believe. There was great passion in him to give meaning to moral life, to grasp history as having purpose, to realize the corelationship between man and God without which he believed man was reduced to skepticism and relativism. Monotheism is truth; from this truth we begin to think and to do. Here is the source of our hope. Monotheism is not compromisable. The moral universe is dependent upon it. It demands courage; to put it extremely, it separates life from death. We would say that it is the deepest and most precious idea of the human spirit. It proclaims the uniqueness of God. In the secret of God's uniqueness lies the reality and purpose of man's capacity to think, act, and feel. This uniqueness embraces every human activity in obligation and freedom. Not myth, nor determinism, but responsibility, courage, and truthfulness structure human activity.

Deeply aware that words can be mere puffs of smoke meaning and saying little, Cohen knew that they had to be embodied in institutions. Truthfulness is, indeed, a grandiose term, but it is the core of family life. If we admit that the family is at the base of societal existence, the distortion of truthfulness on this level is its distortion on all other levels.

> With the establishment of the community of children, Plato, in his *Republic,* destroyed, even more than by his community of women, the psychological foundation of faithfulness in the souls of the human beings who are citizens of his state. If children no longer recognize their own father and mother, it is much worse for them than when parents are not permitted to recognize their own children. In the gratitude of the child's mind, faithfulness establishes the health of the family, and in it the health of every human community.[25]

The family is the source of moral and intellectual instruction. Here the images which we carry with us throughout our lives are formed and developed. Traditions of learning are carried from family to family and from generation to generation. We gather a sense of faithfulness which accompanies learning and embraces courage and prudence. It would be hard to believe that commitment to reason, to community, to our fellow man, is possible without faithfulness to traditions with which these commitments are embodied. There is in us a deep need not only to believe, but also to trust, and it is this trust which is nurtured and formed in learning, in the moral character of the teacher, and, above all, in the examples of the parents. The trust and courage which we deem to be so significant in moral and intellectual life are not learned from books or lectures; they are part of our biological growth, and it is for this reason that Cohen believed that no discussion of a philosophy of history is meaningful without the study of the meaning of virtue. I would not be hesitant to say that the most vital part of Cohen's work on religion is his study of the role that virtue plays in our comprehension of the symbol of Israel as the historical people living with divine commandment. Courage, justice, truthfulness, faithfulness are the homes in which we learn what it means to be committed to monotheism. Without the virtues the idea of humanity, monotheism, would be hollow terms and Cohen's *Ethics* and *Religion of Reason* would have been two more books piled on the heap of others given over to pious ideas. We must first learn how to be moral at home, in school, at work, wherever and whenever we are with our fellow men. Faced with corruption and distortion, with a Hobbesian world, our moral character is not shaped by the slogans we use, but by the upbringing we have had, by the traditions we have lived with, by the people we have associated with and the sensitivity we have developed and felt toward faithfulness and truthfulness. Cohen knew that a people are committed who have learned to value commitment in family and society, in their historical behavior and experience.

The crown of ethical and religious life is peace. Cohen remarks: "What is the epitome of human life in the spirit of the Bible? It is peace. All the meaning, all the value of life is in peace. Peace is the unity of all vital powers, their equilibrium and the reconciliation of all their contradictions. Peace is the crown of life."[26] Cohen identified peace with eternity, the guide of human life. Peace is not to be projected to a world other than ours, diminishing the validity of our moral action and the value of our existence. This dualism would never be acceptable to Cohen. Eternity can be experienced here in the struggle of the pure will, in freedom from fatalism and pessimism. Eternity is experienced in hope, courage, and faith. It is not less felt in learning, in the truthfulness and faithfulness alive in the just act. We experience it in humility and modesty. Peace is in the actions which flow from virtue. It is their harmony; it is the purpose of their being.

The last sentence of Leo Strauss's introduction to the translation of Cohen's *Religion of Reason* states: "It is a blessing for us that Hermann Cohen lived and wrote."[27] If we study the history of the School of Marburg we know how little Cohen was studied at the school he loved so dearly. Hans-Georg Gadamer bears witness to this in his recent autobiography, *Philosophische Lehrjahre*,[28] where the name Cohen appears merely for background purposes. Apart from his influence on Ernst Cassirer, Julius Guttmann, Hugo Bergman, and Eugène Fleischmann, we could say that his works remain without readers. My purpose has been to explore Cohen's attempt to comprehend the meaning of Israel from within the Idealism which was always for him the philosophical side of monotheism. Every philosopher seeks meaning and discourse. Cohen's discourse belongs to his commitment to a moral universe and its embodiment in monotheism. The philosophy of history today still exercises great interest among Christian theologians. The works of Henri de Lubac, Hans Urs von Balthasar, and Gaston Fessard are but a few which are devoted to the meaning of history. Cohen's attempt from the sources of Judaism is the unique achievement of modern Jewish philosophy. Perhaps some have turned away from Cohen's book because they would conceive it to be a partisan effort. It is not. Cohen never yielded to religion, autonomy: "The share religion has in reason binds it to ethics. The methodological connection with ethics has always been the compass of Jewish religion."[29] Cohen laid the foundations not only for our ability to comprehend the relation between ethics and religion, but he made it possible to seek a universal language in and through which philosophies and religions throughout our world could communicate with each other. The embodiment of the religious heritage in the moral law is the source for our continuous search in every religious tradition for those forms and symbols which could make this universal dialogue a reality. The need for communication can only come through philosophy in the purest and simplest form: the search for knowledge, i.e., for meaning. The impulse for this search is the heightened dignity of man, for that deeper discovery of reason and will which he finds in him. From Cohen's last work we perceive the possibility of an ecumenical perspective whose basic impulse is the breakthrough to the universal. From the universal and from universability we can begin to speak again of the significance and value of a philosophy of religion. There is truth in Leo Strauss's words, but it is also a truth which shows us why Cohen was so profoundly neglected by those who came after him in Marburg and by the larger community of philosophers who were no longer the "watchmen" of the moral law. Philosophy and religion belong to each other. "No religious truthfulness can be established exclusively on authoritarian faith; for through this the authority of reason would be renounced, which, together with truthfulness of knowledge, cannot be denied. For the prophetic consciousness also, God's truth is established upon the knowledge of God's holiness, hence upon His moral legislation."[30] The universal discourse of reason belongs as much to the truthfulness of religion as to the essence of philosophy. If peace is the watchword of human life, then its universal truth must be explored and elaborated in that universal discourse of philosophy and religion which joins what is separated, which bridges what is now uncrossable. The meaning of Cohen's last efforts at a religion of reason is the ecumenical embrace which the discourse of reason implies. Yet we know that no such embrace is possible without faith, that capacity of our being which allows us to carry forward the moral and intellectual task which the Ideal prescribes, to comprehend that our ideas function effectively only as beliefs. Yes, we could say with Cohen, "eternity is eternal task, the task of eternity. Heaven and earth may disappear but morality remains."[31] The moral remains *the* essential problem; in its universality the moral content of world religions finds the universability of communication. Every particular moment of this universality affects man with joy, with that sense of being moved which overcomes him before the moral law. Here religious consciousness and aesthetic power become one. The depths of feeling and the awe before the moral law are one with the divine breath which flows upon mankind.

2

Monotheism and History: The Heritage of Hermann Cohen

At the age of seventy the philosopher Hermann Cohen moved from Marburg to Berlin and began to give courses at the Lehranstalt für die Wissenschaft des Judentums. Cohen died six years later in 1918. His fame as head of the School of Marburg brought students from Russia, Spain, the United States to this small German town. Here thundered the great expounder of Kant's philosophy and from there emerged a System of Philosophy: Logic, Ethics, and Aesthetics; the philosopher exploring and elucidating the foundations *Grundlegungen* or *Ideen* of reason, discovering its autonomy, relating the history of this discovery from Plato to Descartes to Leibniz and finally Kant, never ignoring those others in whom we comprehend the perennial attempt to bring to self-consciousness the hidden sources of man's experience, their foundations, and their validity. This commitment to reason at work in man's pursuit of knowledge, the nature of the pure will, and the feeling of beauty had a religious intensity which revealed Cohen's belief in reason as that divine spark which linked man to the idea of humanity and to God as the principle of truth. Never for a moment could or would Cohen question the validity of reason, for that would tear apart the unity and universality of truth, i.e., of God, whose truth man experienced in reason and its manifestations. This was man's unique distinction, to be the bearer of reason and the source of its realization. Not only was reason revealed through man, but in reason man becomes conscious of himself, the discoverer of the meaning of humanity in and through himself. But a philosophy of autonomous reason is the expression of universality and universability which has not yet found space for man as individuality, for the God who is not only the guarantor of our humanity, but who is the object of our longing, the God of the Psalmist. In 1912 Cohen moved closer to the God discovered in prayer, who we not only love but who loves and fills the love with which He is loved. God is *Einzigkeit,* a notion which expresses God's complete otherness. He alone is reality. Cohen, hesitatingly, but surely, moved from philosophy to religion, from the abstract and theoretical God of ethics to the God we long for in prayer and love.

The six years from 1912 to 1918 were decisive for Cohen. From the town of Marburg and its reputation as a world center of Kant studies, to Berlin and the Institute for the Study of Judaism, there emerged more than a geographical shift, but not a repudiation, of Cohen's thought. In two books—*The Concept of Religion in the System of Philosophy* (1915) and *Religion of Reason out of the Sources of Judaism* (1919; 2nd ed. 1929)—we begin to trace this attempt to give religion a distinct relationship to and in the System of Philosophy. The comprehension of this very otherness of God over against man and nature makes it possible to clarify Him as *der Einziger,* who alone is the bearer and guarantor of Being.[1] In the concept of God is His being.[2] The search for the God of the Psalmist, the core of Cohen's activities in Berlin, marks a serious deviation from Marburg, i.e., from philosophy and its autonomy, a genuine development which is necessitated by philosophy. In the depth of his being man knows that God is not a philosophical creation, but that He alone is reality. He alone is the concept of origin, *Ursprungsbegriff.* The question to which there can never be a satisfactory answer is whether these six years and two books are something more than a personal religious adventure of a philosopher who needed more than the autonomous reason, who felt the necessity of prayer, the burning of love, and the peace of the Sabbath in all its social, economic, and political significance and consequences. The love which Cohen had for philosophy he grasped as the gift of God. Cohen moved closely to a practical comprehension of a divinely ordered moral universe. Here, from this universe there arose a confidence in the future, the realization that montheism had only just begun its universal historical development. The past was short, in no way controlling or suffocating. The future is the true dimension of time, prepared for and awakened in the past and present. Messianic hope and vision gave a religious and moral dimension to human activity and responsibility. It broke the hold of mythology. It reinforced that intimate link between love and knowledge, between action and faith. Deep within this commitment to the future was the personal relationship between man and God, that correlation in which man discovered his theomorphic reality: his opening to God, the strength which flowed forth from his longing to be close to the divine.

What is so difficult to comprehend in Cohen is the deepening of the divine-human confrontation and the struggle to achieve the personal vocabulary needed to give it its uniqueness faced with the continuing influence of theoretical terms which drive us back into the speculative experience of philosophy. The tone of Cohen's last book begins with the ringing cry of Akiba at the end of *Mishnah Yoma*. "Blessed are ye oh Israel: before whom do ye make yourselves clean and who makes you clean? It is your father in heaven." The conceptual language of philosophy never loses its right to assert its competence, and when Cohen speaks of the love of God which is rooted in the love which comes from Him, he speaks of the love that only the Idea awakens in us. "How can man love an Idea? The answer: How can man love anything else but the Idea. In sensual love we love only the idealised person, only the idea of the person."[3] The idea of the love of God as the highest ethical reality can indeed arouse love in us, a love which is expressed in *Teshuvah*, the need to re-create ourselves in the security and certainty of God's forgiveness. For Akiba, God is the father before whom we cleanse ourselves and who cleanses us; for Cohen he is father but also the idea of father. Two realities seem to stand alongside each other. Not only the depth of the experience of self in humility and inadequacy before the divine, but also the comprehension of this experience is fundamental for Cohen. Knowledge and love were for him inseparable; he knew the dangers of their separation. To speak of the love of the Idea and of the love of God is to speak of an inseparable reality if we want to avoid the mysticism which allows too intimate an embrace between God and man. The love of God sends man with renewed strength and confidence into the world of social and political action. God's creation is the moral responsibility of every man committed to the belief that creation and revelation depend upon man's actions and purposes. The love which is commanded by God to be directed toward Him is explicable in the fact that the self, which must and should love to be the self, is commanded to do so because of God's infinite love. The power and will to realize the divinely established moral order of creation is possible only when the self, in love, acts with the courage and will developed in the commandment of love. Cohen achieves the breakthrough to the self in the realization that the commandment to love God is the source in which the self is born.

The consequences of the birth of the self is the clear and forceful comprehension of the God of love as the unique God of mankind. The further consequence is the meaning of the Sabbath. "In the Sabbath we come to know the fullness of the divine love."[4] "In the Sabbath the God of love comes forth as the unique God of human love."[5] In the Sabbath an equality fills mankind, a sympathy with suffering, the personal griefs and deep concerns of individuals are brought together and given peace. The Sabbath is the realization of messianic peace. If Judaism had given to mankind only the Sabbath it would have brought the most significant symbol of peace and joy. The mission of monotheism is to fill the earth, to deepen and expand its meaning, to make known the true and efficacious comprehension of the love of man among the peoples of the earth. If there is a breakthrough in history it is that of monotheism and its messianic hope of a universal Sabbath. "This divine love is the guiding star of world history whose meaning man ought not doubt."[6] To know that this history has just begun, "Die Weltgeschichte hat kaum erst angefangen; noch nicht dreitausend Jahre ist sie alt seit Moses und den Propheten."[7] If religion is given a sublime mission, as Cohen now gives it, then it is the curse of montheism which has just begun to break through into human history with its optimism, grandeur of purpose, and its proclamations of the domination of future over past and present. It rejects fate, evil, and the destructive power of cultural pessimism. At the center of this theology of history is divine love expressed in the Sabbath; the messianic dream of the oneness of mankind born in compassion for suffering. "Monotheism is the true trust in history."[8] It implies a sense of destiny which must and should impel the great religious vision. For Cohen this vision embodied the ever-deepening comprehension of God's love for man in which human suffering was redeemed. Each man, whatever be his social, economic, or political condition, is God's concern; in the lowliest dwelling the dignity and welfare of the individual is confirmed. Cohen had a profound sense of the social consequences of God's love. Love means nothing without social consequence. Vastly different from the limitations imposed upon this relationship by those who would and could only speak of their particular and distinct relationship, Cohen's ethical universalism became the space in which God's love flowed over the personal and individual into the political and economic. Divine love is the source of man as a social, economic, and political being. The personal must have wider implications; it is incomprehensible without the societal. God's love is the birth of human rights. "Sie brachte ihm auch seine Ehre wieder und sein Menschenrecht in seiner niedrigen Hütte."[9]

The joy and peace of the Sabbath arise from the contemplation of the fulfillment of creation, of the end of injustice, and of the monotheistic mission that will someday spread to all men and reconcile the truth of God with his creation. The Sabbath is a moment of eternity that breaks forth into the profane. It corresponds to the ethical sublimity which Cohen enunciated in the concept of humanity and which he filled with humaneness. Cohen was always sensitive to the consequential social dimensions of his ethical thought. This concept of humanity would make it possible to struggle against the atavism and racism which he believed were so closely connected with sexual perversity.[10] Cohen knew that any violation of the idea of humanity for the sake of racial distinctions, the notion of superior and inferior races, the purity of blood, the belief in the holiness of land, perverted the morals of a people, infected their notion of sexual relationships because "inferior" peoples became utilizable objects of pleasure. The idea of humanity in the person is perverted; this violation is the source of pessimism, myth, and hate, that violent disbelief in the future, that utter rejection of universality and universability. Most significant and vital from our point of view is the pessimism that refuses a belief in world history that has its source in monotheism, the belief in the incomparability of God, in the fact that he is the source of all reality. This fact that God is the source of reality denies the possibility that any concrete or theoretical given, be it the state, an ideology, a social or economic theory, becomes absolute, self-evident, or universal. The world-historical struggle for monotheism is inseparable from ethical universalism, the trust in the idea of humanity, the belief that God's uniqueness, His love of man, calls forth in us a humaneness, a sensitivity to economic and social suffering and to arbitrary inequality. Monotheism is a destiny, a religious determinant of history which links suffering and love. Suffering born in love and love deepened in suffering. This must be understood on the historical dimension; the bond which ties love and suffering is that which reveals the "sufferings of love." The sufferings which embrace that love for God, for the dignity of our fellow man, and for the pity we show to our fellow being make us more and more aware that the movement of mankind toward the idea of humanity is one of purification. The movement is at its beginnings, and a comprehension of world history necessitates the realization that this beginning embodies the Idea in its fullness and imposes upon man and mankind its concrete expression. Cohen conceived of Israel as the bearer of this Idea, her sufferings are those of the lover whose beloved is joy and pain, hope and disillusion.

The Sabbath is the moment of eternity, the breakthrough to the messianic age, the critique of profanity, the enunciation of truth as divine love, the revelation of God as the source of nature and man; His separability from all that is created. He calls forth from creation purpose, from man responsibility and moral task. Cohen refused to allow the personal dimension to embody the full meaning of this correlation between God's love and his creation. Israel is the center of his world-historical perspective. Cohen's profundity lies in his denial that God-man, man-God correlation is adequate, and it is this denial which gives his philosophy such fundamental importance. World history is a collective responsibility and task. The collective world of Israel, of mankind is needed. The meaning of monotheism and its destiny does not lie in individuals alone. Israel is God's dialogic partner. Here emerges the universality and universability which is the expression of mankind, humanity, humaneness. The dialogue between Israel and God, a dialogue of love and suffering, "the sufferings of love," reveals the eternal mission of monotheism; to transform through knowledge and justice the incompleteness of creation into messianic humanity.

Cohen believed deeply in man's capacity to sanctify both body and soul, to refuse every mythology that threatened the efficacy of the moral obligation, every pessimism that could and would call it into doubt. There can be no philosophy or theology of history where man's capacity for ethical responsibility is challenged or weakened. The drama of history in which the realization and development of monotheism are the central theme is only possible where the belief of reason remains unquestioned and where the hope of the future is the dominating reality of man's comprehension of time. The future neither crushes nor eliminates the past or the present, it transfigures them into the future of possibility. Man becomes a member not of an abstract humanity, but of a peoplehood with a sense of moral power, with the realization that they are creators of history and of a moral spiritual world. The creative powers of man develop from the challenge which is manifested in God's love; in the fact that the movement of the world has meaning only insofar as it stands before God as judge, as the source of social and economic justice, as the beloved toward whom we long to approach, but with whom we are never to be one. The correlation between Israel and God is a reality that enlarges and enhances the moral task. Cohen knew in the depths of his belief that this moral task borne collectively by Israel would bring a new future inspired by a new hope. There is an optimism in the growing moral and spiritual awareness of the Idea of God. This is an optimism which gathers its strength from the negation which existence presents and which history seems to justify. This defiance of existence is not irrational; it does not confirm a blindness to the passions, a refusal to recognize man's inhumanity and worship of power. This optimism has a world-historical dimension; it is the optimism of monotheism, the belief that the past is not controlling, that the beginning of the spiritual struggle has had only a short history, and that what we have affirmed about human nature is preliminary and inadequate. Man's universe is growing and will continue to develop. *The creation has only just begun;* this process of growth and change is fundamental for our understanding of God's love. This love undergoes no process or change, but our capacity to grasp and be grasped by it belongs to history, to the growing nature of the universe and our place in it. The breakthroughs of love heal that division between the holy and the profane, between the material and the spiritual. In Israel Cohen witnessed this healing and knew that with the history of Judaism, the history of religion was beginning its struggle against mythology. Monotheism has not yet transformed the world; its revolutionary nature is still to be experienced. Monotheism is revolutionary. It sets aside every polytheism, every identification of truth with nature and human existence. It rejects pantheism and necessitates the eternal and holy ethical demand for humanity and universality, the real separation of the profane and the holy, experienced in daily life, in the religious calendar, in prayer, and in messianic hope.

Peace is the ultimate reconciliation of creation; it is the meaning of the Messiah, the messianic age; it is Israel's message and her martyrdom, i.e., her "sufferings of love." In her religious celebrations moments of this peace are enjoyed; there is a freedom from the anxiety of self-preservation. The individual lives the reconciliation that is the essence of the religious ideal and hope. This reconciliation neither weakens nor annuls the infinite task of ethics, the responsibility to realize in nature moral responsibility and universality, to posit the future as the idea of eternity, providing no conclusion, no concrete end to the ethical task. To be yoked to the Law is for Cohen citizenship in the Kingdom of God. This citizenship is man's freedom; to bear the law as obligation is no longer to wander aimlessly through the world creating imaginary hopes and dreams of unencountered reality. Man's freedom begins in receptivity to God's law; to grasp the meaning of life is no longer an arbitrary act of will, which becomes slavery and nihilism, but responsibility for creation, a response to God's love, an embracing of the Kingdom of God within the self. For Cohen, Israel announces this Kingdom, this is her truth, the truth which is her "imperial message." She announces the Kingdom of peace, the ultimate and supreme consequence of correlation. The consequence is Cohen's philosophy of history. History begins with God and is carried forth and revealed by Israel, by every individual who willingly accepts the eternal being of ethics, citizenship in the Kingdom of God, who willingly receives the task and responsibility of the Law. Cohen's imagery and visions made it possible for him to comprehend Israel as the symbolic actualization of the messianic hope for redemption. The imagination does not bring about a series of conceptualizations, but imputes communication through the assumption that men freely employing their imagination would and could concur in their comprehension of these symbols. Cohen's belief in the world-historical significance of monotheism and its embodiment in Israel's divine historical mission depended upon a "free play" of the imagination. This "free play," however, is correlated to the belief which Cohen had in God's love. In Cohen the imagination was enlightened by belief; it was the gift of the God whom he so dearly loved. At every present, a moment of reconciliation between creation and creator is occurring through the mediation of Israel. Peace is the summary of all values; all the paths of virtue find their end in peace. This is the goal of mankind. To philosophize is a religious act. Cohen believed that philosophy and religion could be joined in the love and knowledge of God. Peace is the reconciliation of the temporal and the eternal. Cohen had now found a concept of history intimately linked with the eternity of the ethical task; he discovered that history makes sense as a response to God the Creator, to God's love. Man is not autonomous, he stands under the Law, responsible for the creation in which he comes to understand his dependency and inadequacy, his need for his fellow beings, and his dependency upon God. From Idealism Cohen moved to religion, which he now envisioned as human destiny laden with a profound ethical calling made real in the Idea of humanity and humaneness. The last six years of Cohen's life produced a dramatic development in his System of Philosophy: he found, in addition to the God of the prophets and their universalism, the God of the Psalmist. He found the efficacy of prayer and love. In correlation and copartnership Cohen expressed a philosophy of history in which human and divine realities realized themselves through each other.

In 1920 Gerhard Krueger came to Marburg to study philosophy. Cohen's influence was ignored by his critics, what he had built they were now bringing down. Paul Natorp, no longer overshadowed by Cohen's prophetic powers, found solace in mysticism and music. Nicolai Hartmann and Heinz Heimsoeth were reconstructing Kant in opposition to Cohen's System of Philosophy. In 1923 Heidegger appeared on the scene and with him the last traces of ethical idealism were buried. This radical demolition of Cohen's thought needs explanation and we still await the philosopher or historian to show how from the structure of autonomous reason mythology and irrationalism finally dominated German academic philosophy. The movement away from Cohen was less radical among his Jewish successors with the exception of Martin Buber, who was less a philosopher than a romantic and mystic. Franz Rosenzweig, Ernst Cassirer, and Julius Guttmann remained closer to Cohen. This is always possible when Law, Love, and Commandment maintain their unity, or at least where none of these factors is lost or denied.

One of the most significant works of contemporary German philosophy is Krueger's *Grundfragen der Philosophie* (1958).[11] It is in many ways an introduction to religious and philosophical thought. Before attempting an evaluation of Krueger's concepts of history and God which I believe are central to his philosophy, we should mention a few biographical events. He was born in 1902 and died in 1972. He finished his degree at Marburg in 1929. In 1933 he was at Göttingen and at Frankfurt/Main; he became professor at Frankfurt. From 1940 to 1946 he was professor at Münster and from 1946 to 1952 at Tübingen. Forty years separate the publication of Krueger's *Grundfragen* from Cohen's *Religion of Reason,* years which saw the influence of Marburg in the philosophical perspectives of Heidegger and Hartmann, in those of Rosenzweig and Cassirer, but if we ask ourselves about Cohen's System and its overcoming, its rejection, or the simple fact that it was ignored, we arrive at a simple but factual response: Cohen's philosophy may have been overcome but not eliminated, negated but not destroyed. Without Cohen it is not possible to comprehend his successors. In them Cohen was forgotten, but in this negation and ignorance there is the source of an emergence. We have only just begun to comprehend the significance of Cohen's thought. Karl Löwith has remarked that like Rosenzweig's *Stern,* Cohen's *Religion der Vernunft* remains unknown to the German intellectual world. It is striking that Heidegger, in his report "Zur Geschichte des philosophischen Lehrstuhl der Marburger Universität," does not mention Cohen's *Religion der Vernunft* among its works.[12] More surprising would have been the recognition of this book not only by Heidegger, but by those in the theological faculty, R. Otto or R. Bultmann. The consequences of this failure had made impossible a meaningful evaluation of Cohen in the history of contemporary philosophy, and, in particular, the history of German philosophy in the twentieth century.

At the very beginning of his text Krueger makes two significant statements about history: "We live at a period of total and uncontrolled historical relevance." "The historical relevancy of life has become extreme."[13] The question which is fundamental for Krueger is not that of the true meaning of life, "nicht mehr die Frage nach dem wahren Lebenssinn," but whether there is at all a meaning for life and how it is possible for man to exist in any kind of meaningful way, "ob es überhaupt einen Lebenssinn gibt und wie es möglich ist, als Mensch, d.h. in irgendeiner sinnvollen Weise zu existieren." The questions of history and the possibility of meaning in a world that has been captured and structured by historical relevancy are the ones which Krueger finds fundamental. Man finds himself in the position that he is now given the task of discovering what he is, and must be, in order to call himself a man.[14] A radical separation between world and man has occurred as the consequence of the attempt of man to embody in himself an autonomy which excludes dependence and what Cohen would call corelationship. Krueger makes a decisive critique of German Idealism:

> No less self-sufficient should philosophy be toward our fellow being, *Mitmensch*. The absolute thinker viewed himself as the distinctly true thinker, who needed no critique and assistance from anyone else, not to mention any kind of authority. He valued the philosophy of the most talented thinkers as preliminary steps to his own. Thus, Fichte judged Kant, Schelling Fichte, and Hegel all the others. His philosophy was truth, the unique thinkable measure for all evaluation of knowledge. Fichte, Schelling, and Hegel all thought that their teaching could no longer be threatened by historical destiny.[15]

This autocracy of philosophy is the source of man's alienation and its consequential reduction of life to the domination of historical relevancy. This domination Krueger identifies with relativistic historicism, the thought of Dilthey, Nietzsche, and Troeltsch. The autocracy which Krueger sees in Fichte, Schelling, and Hegel removes philosophy from the creation. Now it is the source of creation. Removed from the need of our fellow man, it claims spontaneity and self-sufficiency. Its reason is no longer from God; it no longer participates in creation but creates. What are the consequences for man?—the estrangement of man from nature, community, society. There is no need for a unifying meaning of life. Man is independent of all dependence.

The last period of Cohen's life, those six years in Berlin, were decisive for his concepts of correlation and copartnership. Krueger's life had no such development. From his Kant book to his study of Plato in 1939, he was convinced of a reality which Franz Rosenzweig had expressed in the *Star of Redemption:* "Only the soul beloved of God can receive the commandment to love its neighbor and fulfill it. Ere man can turn himself over to God's will, God must first have turned to man."[16] Krueger, who often quoted Augustine, who so deeply embodied Plato's faith and love, knew that in these words of love—"You touched me, and I am inflamed with the love of your peace, tetigisti me, et exarsi in pacem tuam"[17]—the profane and the religious experience found their point of separation. Here we begin to comprehend what Krueger calls the separation of the profane from the religious. What is the reality which excites us, what is the love which moves our love, the light which illumines the light by which we see, the Good which draws us toward it, which awakens our sensitivity and receptivity? Augustine knew that receptivity was the source of spontaneity, he pleaded for that grace that would penetrate and light his darkness. The development of our receptivity begins with the comprehension that as dependent beings we are in need, we long to be embraced, to be filled and grasped, that what comes from the Other awakens in us the capacity to receive. Receptivity emerges from its depths as it moves forth in response to the ennobling and expansive power of divinity. Receptivity emerges in dialogue; it dies in monologue; it expands in mutuality, is diminished in monadic life; it advances toward the Beloved in belief, in the truth and beauty of its Beloved. Receptivity establishes our finiteness and dependency, our indigency and sentiment; it awakens the mediating power of love which moves from God to man and from man to God. Receptivity is for Krueger a finiteness that stands open to eternity. History is this continuous dialogue between the finite and the eternal; it is what gives man's existence meaning, *Lebenssinn,* it establishes the sense of tradition which links man to those philosophical and religious truths which place the meaning of life before eternity. "Man's eternity is implanted in the soul of creation." Rosenzweig's words illuminate what Krueger is attempting to tell us.

> Being loved and living are the two moments of his life, separate from God, yet united in man, and creation would be the And between them. Being loved comes to man from God, loving turns toward the world. How else could they count as one for him? How else could he be conscious of loving God by loving his neighbor if he did not know from the first and the innermost that the neighbor is God's creature and that his love of neighbor is love of the creatures.[18]

The search for meaning is the fundamental endeavor of philosophy and religion. In this struggle to find meaning the consciousness of the interrelationship which must exist between man, creation, and God emerges. Man's thinking takes place within a world that he finds before him and where exists the reality he must discover. It is not a world which he creates, but one that is created. Man thinks and acts in response to what affects him; he thinks with others because he is responsible as a moral being to the community of men. Truth is the given world with its changing and its unchanging form: *das Wandelbare, das Bleibende.*

Krueger has always believed that a religious world experience makes it possible to find an end for our existence. Like philosophy which is the mystery of passionate love, religion forces us to question the meaning of our actions, the justifications of our decisions. It necessitates self-knowledge, the realization of our temporality, and the force which it creates to turn us toward the True, the Good, and the Beautiful. What therefore becomes central is the problem of history and God. What remains permanent is the continuous change of reality. "There is, we can say, not only history but also tradition."[19] Krueger would say that in all the changing there is "a kernel of the changeless, true and universal humanity."[20] This kernel is the truth which breaks into time, the Kairos, and remains the eternal present in time. Rosenzweig elucidates this point when he speaks of the meaning of the eternal Israel.

> Therefore the true eternity of the eternal people must always be alien and vexing to the state, and to the history of the world. . . . So long as the Kingdom of God is still to come, the course of world history will always only reconcile creation within itself, only the moment which is about to come with that which has just passed. Only the eternal people, which is not encompassed by world history, can—at every moment—bind creation as a whole to redemption, while redemption is still to come. The life of this people, alone, burns with a fire which feeds on itself, and hence needs no sword to supply the flame with fuel from the forests of the world.[21]

This notion of the *Knesseth Israel,* the ecclesia of Israel, is that eternal reality which Krueger identifies with Platonic philosophy in particular, the realization that there is an absolute, nonhistorical confrontation with truth, a light which lights the light which is in us, which denies the possibility of sovereign freedom, but affirms freedom in relation to authority and tradition, freedom in terms of the law: "Tradition in philosophy, the metaphysical truth which since Socrates, Plato and

Aristotle has never ceased to claim our thinking."[22] This truth is the "monotheistic cosmos" which these philosophers have revealed to us; it is a truth which has never parted from our remembrances, the source of the continuity of this tradition. The Greeks have a fundamental meaning for us; in them there was a "breakthrough" to eternity. If it be the ecclesia of Israel, the philosophy of Plato, or the mystical body of Christ, the search for the eternal is *the* problem of philosophy and religion, inspired and permeated by the Greek tradition. This tradition was as precious to Krueger as eternal Israel was to Cohen and Rosenzweig.

Platonism had a magisterial authority for Krueger. If philosophy taught us how to think in response to God, then it is Plato who teaches us that thinking and loving are inseparable. We are compelled to find meaning outside of ourselves in order to be able to find it within ourselves. Philosophy is an elaboration of an original experience, of man's confrontation with a power that is beyond him and to which he respondes in love. If man values his reality, if he becomes conscious of its meaning, is it then possible for him to avoid the *Urerfahrung* which brings together the power of being grasped, which is receptivity, and that divine truth which opens and expands this power as it approaches and illuminates it? The deepest human sentiment only unveils the sharp truth that man cannot be objective toward what he thinks. He comes to know only in the passion of love. Passion is the source of thinking. We only know what we can love; we grasp because we are grasped. This truth became clearer to Cohen in his last two books; it was fundamental to Rosenzweig, who offers us a profound commentary on the commandment: "Thou shalt love the Lord thy God with all thy heart and with all thy soul and with all thy might." It is a paradoxical commandment because it is obvious that love cannot be commanded. But God does command it.

> The commandment to love can only proceed from the mouth of the lover. Only the lover can and does say: love me!—and he really does so. In his mouth the commandment to love is not a strange commandment; it is none other than the voice of love itself. The love of the lover has, in fact, no other word to express itself than the commandment. . . . But the "Love me!" of the lover—that is wholly perfect expression, wholly pure language

of love. . . . The commandment knows only the moment; it awaits the result of the very instant of its promulgation.[23]

Here the command to love is the awakening of self, the root of that partnership between man and God; it is what Krueger would call the "state of being grasped" and what Cohen comprehended in the dialogue with the God of the Psalmist. Deep within all the attempts to discover man's relationship with a Being outside himself we discover what Krueger calls *dienstbare Freiheit,* serving freedom. "World history rests upon human freedom, but not upon a creative freedom with which man himself first designed the world and created a cosmos from a chaos of given objects."[24] History is fundamentally the history of religion. The profane world view is service to false gods, *Dienst an falschen Göttern.* These are no longer the gods of Olympus or of the Underworld, they are the gods born from what Krueger calls the *Katastrophe Hegels.* These are the ones that emanate from man's assumption of sovereignty over the heavens and the earth. In that clear and precise critique of Hegel, Krueger said: "Seine Philosophie war ja die Wahrheit Selbst."[25] In this claim to truth Hegel encompassed God in philosophy; the philosopher was above history, independent, adequate, and free in his magisterial autocracy. Krueger's meditation on history convinced him that man "is not creator, and not master of the world," cannot change the fact that things are as they are. He can comprehend himself only as part of the creation, morally responsible for its preservation. He experiences religion as the original consciousness of a closeness to God. Julius Guttmann, close to the thought of Hermann Cohen, described religion as "the yearning to bridge the gap between God and man, which has been caused by sin; religion rejoices in the light of God's face, and now has the courage to bear life's adversities."[26] God is true Being, the source of being, incomparable to any other being. All these expressions force and necessitate us to comprehend our finiteness, its temporality, and the confrontation with eternity. Man reduced to finitude and temporality takes his place in creation, assumes his creatureliness, and with this bodily identification with all creation makes real the idea of humanity, not only as a spiritual concept, but more important as a bodily concept in which ethical responsibility becomes concrete in suffering and pity, *Mitleid.* Not autonomy and spontaneity but dependence, inadequacy, and the need for our fellow man are the root and source of a philosophical-religious meaning of life.

Similar to Krueger's remark about the *Katastrophe Hegels* was Rosenzweig's opposition to Hegel and Schelling. He shared no sympathy for a metaphysical identity between spirit and nature which historically was realized as the spirit emerged, in and through negation, from consciousness to self-consciousness to reason. Cohen had spoken of *Hegels Fehler,* which was for Cohen the identify of the reasonalbe and the real. Cohen was affronted by the famous Hegelian dictum "Was vernunftig ist, ist wirklich." "In no way," Cohen replied, "is reality the measure and principle of ethical reason. . . . What is reasonable is not real, but it should become real."[27] Heavens separate Kant from Hegel. In both Cohen and Rosenzweig, Krueger could have discovered faithful and friendly predecessors. Guttman clarifies Rosenzweig's position in a way which shows an affinity to that of Krueger's:

> In order that the world be awakened to life and ensoulment, there is a necessity for the work of man, who is different from the world and who stands against it. That the world and man can influence one another is possible only because both originate in God, and the love which man caused to grow in the heart of man still operates the world, and brings the dormant life of the world into development.[28]

It is this origination in God, this identification of God and truth that we experience the mutual dependence of all living beings. The truth of God does not diminish man's activity, it stimulates and necessitates it. Human suffering and joy, the search for meaning and value, the longing for the universality of the divine-human dialogue form the basis of humanity, of the community of human beings who comprehend the responsibility of finiteness and temporality. No being is autonomous or free without the realization of communal and existential dependence. Krueger spoke of the changing and permanent; he could have spoken of the eternal and the historical, fundamentally, the experience of *Ergriffenheit,* that grasping force which is the divine, is the unique ground of the confrontation of man and God. To be grasped by the Reality which is the source of all existence, is to know that truth *is* and all else is becoming.

Ernst Cassirer studied with Cohen at Marburg. He left his position at Hamburg in the spring of 1933 after Hitler had become chancellor in January of the same year. While at Hamburg a young man named Eric Weil came to study philosophy with Cassirer and had before his death in 1977 become one of France's great philosophers. Like Cassirer, he emigrated from Germany but settled in Paris, became a French citizen, and achieved professorships at Lille and at Nice. In 1950 Weil wrote his most significant book, *Logique de la philosophie*. It is in this book, which elaborates the perennial discourse of reason, its categories and their *reprise,* that we find a discussion of the category of God. Cassirer considered religion to be part of man's "symbolic system."

> As compared with other animals man lives not merely in a broader reality; he lives, so to speak, in a new dimension of reality.... No longer can man confront reality immediately; he cannot see it, as it were, face to face. Physical reality seems to recede in proportion as man's symbolic activity advances.[29]

Cassirer found that the symbol became the tool by and through which man could break the power of mythology and taboo. Religion played the essential role because it understood that the symbol not only extended thought but was the vehicle of God's word, his commandment, and his love. In the ethical universality of religion the political myth found its strongest antagonist. Here we can read the history of human culture as the struggle of the ideal and the idea, the universal and the eternal, with the mythical, the demonic attempt to deify the temporal and the given. The *crimen laesae magestatis* of Judaism, its struggle with National Socialism, Cassirer understood as the confrontation of ethical monotheism and the political taboo system. "If Judaism has contributed to break the power of the modern political myth, it has done its duty, having once more fulfilled its historical and religious mission."[30] Cassirer wrote this in 1944, one year before his death. Cohen's meditation on history and the world mission of monotheism is alive in these words. The devotion to the ethical universalism of monotheism is one of the great contributions of the School of Marburg. The growth of the political myth in all forms of totalitarianism makes our understanding of the contribution of Cohen even more essential. Cohen knew that genuine philosophy and religion recognized the radical difference between *Sein* and *Sollen*. "The distinction between *being* and the *ought to be* separates not only two worlds but also the world view of pantheistic metaphysics from the ethical; similarly, of theoretical idealism from the ethics of autonomous law giving, *Selbstgesetzgebung*."[31] The recognition of the separation of the two worlds and the consequent demand that they interact through activity was the Kantian heritage and loyalty of both Cohen and Cassirer. No myth can set aside man's responsibility *to do*.

Where and how does Eric Weil's discussion of God and history enter into the tradition of Cohen, Cassirer, or Krueger? God is a category, He belongs to the philosopher's discourse, and it is from this discourse that Weil attempts to comprehend the meaning of God for man. If we are to speak of the meaning of God for man, then we must find the discourse which makes it possible to speak of God the creator in and through whom man comes to comprehend himself. The category of God is preceded by the category of self and followed by that of condition. Being a category, God belongs to philosophical discourse, and it is within this discourse that man comes to grips with what it means to speak of God, but not what it means to experience Him as the incomparable Other. In God, man finds the other in whom is mirrored his lost perfection, the path, the goal, the purpose of his striving. Through the other, man begins to come to terms with what it means to be man, the being who is fallen, but who finds in this fall the source of his dignity and freedom. If man were not a fallen being, God would not be for him this other in whom he now discovers freedom for obligation. The previous state of beatitude excluded all need for self-comprehension and self-consciousness, no awareness of moral struggle, no need to seek universality. The discovery of the infinite reality which is God, in a situation from which He can be addressed and which He addresses, is man's rediscovery of the intimate and fundamental relationship between the finite and the infinite, between the divine and the human, mediated in love and reason. To this we can add that "man is only man and self where he is not alone."[32] To comprehend that a reality becomes this or that reality only as it is reflected in its other is necessary if we are to grasp Weil's repeated argument that "the life of man is not in himself but in God."[33] What is significant is not the apparent logical formulae that seem to express relationship, but the ethical content of the confrontation between the divine and the human, the passion, tension, pain, and anxiety which it embraces. The relationship unveils man's dependence as the root of his existence. If not elaborated in Augustinian love terminology, it nevertheless seeks to embrace the "sufferings of love" alive in the confrontation between man and God.

It is in the love of God that man's solitude disappears. He shares with his fellow man and with humanity what he calls the fatherhood of man, a symbol in which the human is addressed by the divine and man respondes to this recognition with a new concept of self and responsibility. The symbol becomes a hierophany. Solitude, as unmediated particularity, is the source of man's alienation from himself and his fellow man, in it lies the demonic possibility that particularity may become totality, the possibility that man can always choose the life of the nonbeliever.

> The concrete self disappears in this confrontation with God, and the sacrifice of the heart immolates every particular tradition, law and burns them on the altar of sentiment. God appears in this disappearance of particulars. . . . God is the infinite in face of man who is always determined. It is in destruction through freedom that the determination of freedom exists and God reveals himself in his truth: *in interiore homine habitat veritas* (Augustine, De Trinitate, XIV, 7).[34]

If it is true that the believer sees all reality in God and not in himself, nevertheless he is aware that it is in him that God exists and that his existence is the embodiment of essence. Although the believer continues to live in the world, he now knows that he is recognized. In this knowledge of recognition man is no longer bound to the world of things, he is called to a higher destiny, a theomorphic destiny. In this act of recognition man is born anew. The fact of recognition is that of man's freedom, nothing can now enclose him, control or embody him. Recognition is the awareness of relationship. From the perspective of the discourse of philosophy, man's recognition, his embodiment of the truth, establishes the confrontation of particular and universal as the self-consciousness of man as self and freedom. Man is no longer fated as a natural object, in analogy with God he is free to discover a perennially changing relationship to nature and to his fellow man. Man is free to create symbols, metaphors, and analogies to comprehend the world which he unveils and which unveils him.

Weil believed that the category of God is the "turning point of philosophical becoming."[35] This category is a central moment of the logic of philosophy. In and through this category man initiates a discourse on God embodying no historical revelation and implying no anthropological reduction of God. We speak here of natural theology. In beginning a discourse on God man also commences a discourse on man who thinks the God of man. The discourse on God encompasses the discourse on man. Philosophical discourse is ultimately concerned with the meaning which God has for man, for the meaning he seeks to discover in relation to the world and the purpose of his existence. The question which accompanies this discourse is whether the God that is now a category is not a necessary fiction which philosophy has continuously evoked to comprehend man's need for recognition and purpose. If man finds the world already given and if he discovers reason and its history, does he similarly discover God, or is the divine-human confrontation dependent upon God's love? From the point of view of the philosophical discourse the essential question is not God, but the affect of the concept of God upon man and the resultant discourse. "God is anthropomorphic only for the language of the world and need; man is theomorphic."[36] The gap between God and man is bridgeable, discourse is possible, and although we may not be able to speak of reconciliation, we can speak of man's feelings, of his longing and of his reason, all uniting in a never-ending striving to realize divinity, or we may say, to realize the essence which is embodied in his existence. Man is the image of God, but is only image. Total revelation is man's annihilation. The knowledge of God is the end of man. There is forever a gap between Being and the Ought to Be, but Being is always embodied in the Ought to Be as its infinitesimal possibility. God is always present as the eternity of freedom. That man can be free because God is freedom is the clarion call of man's creativity, which, analogous to God's, allows man to transcend every certitude, truth, self, and object. If the divine-human relationship means anything to man, it signifies for him the refusal to deify his world, the negation of mythology and pantheism, refusal of the claim that being in its immediacy and reification can deny mediation, negation, and transcendence. Negation is here no obstruction, but a living experience. This is what Cohen achieved in moving from the theoretical abstractness of reason to God as the source of creation and revelation. Rosenzweig moved in the same direction. In the Introduction to the *Star* he remarked:

He [Cohen] replaced the one and universal Naught, *Nichts,* that veritable "no thing" *Unding* which, like a zero *Null* really can be nothing more that "nothing," with the particular Naught which burst fruitfully into reality. There he took his stand in most decided opposition precisely to Hegel's founding of logic on the concept of Being, and thereby in turn to the whole philosophy in whose inheritance Hegel had come. For here for the first time a philosopher who himself still considered himself an "Idealist" recognized and acknowledged that what confronted reasoning when it set out in order "purely to create" was not Being but Naught.[37]

Cohen achieved a breakthrough of Idealism, as Rosenzweig hoped, because he believed the creation bears within it becoming and its concept, but he refused to accept the idea that Becoming and Being were commensurate. The incomparable nature of God is the origin of becoming, *der Ursprung*. Becoming and its origin are not one. Becoming does not exhaust its origin; it is contingent to it.

Weil believed that the idea of God liberates man from servitude to the world of appearances. He is the thought which forces man to see through appearance to its sources. Pierre Fruchon, commenting on Weil's category of God, states: "God is not originally a representation which enslaves, but thought which liberates, which allows man to comprehend himself in his free humanity."[38] The discourse of man on God is the freedom which is man's to search for meaning, to seek for the meaning of what it is to say that God is the creator of the world. Man's philosophical concern is the problem of meaning, how to elaborate a reasonable comprehension of creation. If God is the continuous source of creation, then man is the perennial source of its meaning. The ever-renewed creation is the ground of man's constant struggle to elaborate meaning in symbols and metaphors. If the creation could be comprehended, then man would be its master and the knower of God. With this knowledge man would no longer be man, fallible and dependent. In such a world, man as such has no role; for where man need exercise no action and decision, he can find no meaning for his life. His faith is that God *is,* that he, man, is free because the world is renewed each day. Man's search for God is analogous to man's search for meaning. The category of God awakens in man the meaning of the potentiality of reason and the reasonable, freedom and moral responsibility, the obligation to give meaning to life and to the world in which he dwells. Nevertheless, man remains in a world which he does not fully comprehend, and in which such ideas as justice and virtue appear to have little relation to reality. The course of history and the idea of a divinely grounded moral order do not correspond. This conflict between reality and morality is at the core of morality, the challenge to both thinking and willing. The thinking which embraces this radical gap between Being and the Ought to Be is necessarily circular. The problem emerges again and again as we comprehend more deeply the Ought to Be and realize the resistance of amoral nature. "In no way," Cohen said, "does moral reason coincide with reality; the moral law with the historical reality of the law and the state."[39] In one of Weil's last essays, "Faudra-t-il de nouveau parler de morale?"[40] he clearly separates historical reality and morality. He speaks of philosphical faith, the faith that philosophers must accept a *wager* and must believe without knowing "because without such faith, and from another perspective, without such hope, the question of meaning can never even be posed. . . ."[41] If it is correct to assume that Weil was closer to Kant than to Hegel, then we see in this last expression of his moral view a position closer to Cohen than he was aware of or willing to admit. At the deepest level of Cohen's ethics, and its permeation by prophetic moralism, there lived that holy and necessary separation between *Sein* and *Sollen*. If monotheism is man's sublime ethical mission, then the duality between reality and reason is fundamental. At the core of every thinker whose roots are in biblical prophetic morality this dualism assumes a constant and challenging commitment.

Hermann Cohen's philosophy has been negated, denied, overcome, but in a deeper sense its comprehension is just beginning. If we read it in Cassirer, Krueger, Rosenzweig, and even in Weil, we feel that it remains powerful and determining wherever and whenever we face and confront the meaning of moral reality, the implication of the moral command, its universality, and its divine sanction. Cohen believed that God is the source of reality, that man's reason is created and partakes in divinity, not autonomous but dependent, not self-sufficient but indigent and inadequate. Human reality begins in correlation. Hugo Bergman has remarked that: "The correlation between God and man is characterized by what the Jewish tradition calls *ruah hakodesh,* the

Spirit of Holiness. The 'holy spirit' is *between* man and God, not *in* either. It is not an attribute of either God or man, but of their relation."[42] This notion of correlation and copartnership is rooted in Cohen's acceptance of man as a "co-worker in the work of creation." This notion presupposes two movements: 1) man turns to God in repentance, and 2) man's belief in God's forgiveness. The religious dimension not only gives man a share in the work of creation, but "man's specific creative responsibility is the establishment of the one, messianic mankind. A united mankind cannot be the product of nature; nature created 'man' but not 'mankind.'"[43]

We have attempted to show that Cohen's ethical and religious thought, although ignored in the German academic world, has remained the fundamental philosophy of thinkers who have desired to come to terms with ethics and history, rooted in the belief that God is the source of reality. The problem does not change; it requires deeper and ongoing reflection. This means that Cohen must be studied again. From his philosophy we can comprehend the course of the history of Marburg: irrationalism, existentialism, rationalism. Without Cohen it is difficult to grasp the directions of Natorp, Heidegger, and Hartmann, of Cassirer, Krueger, Rosenzweig, and Buber, not to mention the theologians Otto and Bultmann. The history of these paths has yet to be written, but before it is attempted its center, Hermann Cohen, must be understood. We can assume that Rosenzweig was correct when he stated that Cohen stood in direct opposition to Hegel's founding of logic on the concept of Being, and began instead with *das besondere Nichts*. With this assumption and Cohen's belief that God is the *einzig Sein* and therefore the origin, *Ursprung,* of becoming, we can comprehend his refusal to accept the concept of a "ground of emanation." The refusal implied that the "ground of emanation" was for Cohen mythological. "God's positive determination is in those negative attributes which do not exclude positivity, but privation,"[44] i.e., they emerge from the perennial negation of privation. The heritage of Cohen belongs to that clear and distinct separation between Being and the Ought to Be, between the real and the reasonable, and to the qualitative difference between future and present. If in myth there is no clear demarcation between past, present, and future; in the messianic vision and hope of monotheism the separation is precise and demarcated. Cohen leaves us with belief, mission, and history. We must come to terms with our spiritual and bodily finiteness and with the fact that our reason is created but nevertheless partakes of the creator. The search for meaning is inseparable from God and history, from that distinction between God's renewal of creation and man's struggle to find meaning in a creation which is to remain forever incomplete, inadequate, and insufficient. The consequence of God's love is man's limited and dependent freedom.

Our last remarks refer to Cohen's statement that the "ground of emanation" is mythological. Kant had already stated that ethical freedom is not a fact but a postulate, it is not given, but is a task. If freedom is not a given of our nature, then to fulfill this task we cannot depend upon the natural development of our nature, but only upon a free rational act of the will in contradition to our nature. Nature, if followed, would lead us to dependence upon the natural order, to the denial of personal responsibility. The incomparable Being of God is the possibility of our freedom. In relation to Him the creation is not completed but is renewed at every moment of becoming, "a new beginning" is made with every act of human freedom, with man as the "bearer of reason and as the rational essence of morality." This "new beginning" is the sharpest and severest contradiction to every attempt to reduce man and history to the "spindle of necessity," to mythical thinking. Each on her throne, the Fates, daughters of necessity, "Lachesis and Clotho and Atropos sang in unison with the music of the sirens. Lachesis singing of things that were, Clotho the things that are, and Atropos the things that are to be."[45] Caught in the stream of time, powerless to alter our human situation, we are destined to accept the conditions of our existence, analyze and elaborate its fateful nature. Here philosophical and mythological thought separate. Philosophy thinks against time, it believes in the world of "eternal truth" and this belief becomes a trust. Philosophy returns to mythology when it loses its belief in the "realm of ideas," when it remains embedded in condition which it accepts as unchangeable, and from which it now attempts to discover and define man. Philosophy begins at that moment when we recognize that moral reason and reality do not coincide. Here we find the mission of monotheism: man's correlation to and partnership with God, man's assumption of the Kingdom of God as the messianic destiny of mankind. In this relationship man is created anew, before God has made a "new beginning." With courage and hope he is open to the future and its promise.

At the end of his book *The Myth of the State,* Cassirer warns us against taking lightly the political myths which we find "absurd, incongruous, fantastic and ludicrous." "We should carefully study the origin, the structure, the methods and the technique of political myths."[46] In the heritage of Hermann Cohen, the struggle for our culture has always implied an opposition to and a struggle against atavism, nationalism, and cultural pessimism. Cohen was a watchman of the divinely grounded moral order of being. He left his watchmanship to his fellow philosophers. Most slept, others ignored, and those awake had to flee the emergence of totalitarianism. We read this history with sadness and melancholy, but knowing that Cohen still has influence, we have hope. Cassirer, writing in 1944 of Heidegger and Spengler, said:

> As soon as philosphy no longer trusts its own power, as soon as it gives way to a merely passive attitude, it can no longer fulfil its most important educational task.... A philosophy which indulges in somber predictions about the decline and the inevitable destruction of human culture, a philosophy whose whole attention is focused on the *Geworfenheit*, the Being-thrown of man, can no longer do its duty.[47]

Duty, as ethical responsibility, as breakthrough to universality and universability, is the responsibility of human freedom standing before God as commandment.

3

Time and History: The Conflict between Hermann Cohen and Franz Rosenzweig

The idea of time distinguishes the philosophy of Hermann Cohen from that of Franz Rosenzweig. We accept the judgment of Cohen's student Ernst Cassirer that Cohen "of all modern thinkers has felt this fundamental idea of the Prophetic religion most deeply and renewed it in the greatest purity." In Cohen's own words: "Time becomes future and only future. Past and present are submerged in this time of the future. This return to time is the purist idealization. Before this idea, all existence vanishes. The existence of man is transcended in this future being."[1] Thus, the thought of history as the conflict between the real and the ideal becomes meaningful for the life of man and the nations. Rosenzweig is no longer concerned with this conflict in the Kantian-Cohenian sense. He is inspired by Schelling and his speculations about cosmic time, mythology, and eternity. "The Jew alone suffers no conflict between the supreme vision which is placed before his soul and people among whom his life has placed him. He alone possesses the unity of myth which the nations lost through the influx of Christianity. . . . The Jew's myth, leading him into his people, brings him face to face with God who is also the God of all nations."[2] Two distinct conceptions of time and history bear different consequences, and it is these which this chapter intends to explore and evaluate. No attempt to deal with this subject would be possible without a serious comprehension of Eugène Fleischmann's *Christianity Revealed*,[3] through which we come to understand how deeply Schelling influenced Rosenzweig's search to find the ground of the subjective character of time. "Rosenzweig found by chance at an old book dealer Schelling's fragments which were published with the title *The Ages of the World* [1811] and these gave him all that he wanted."[4] If we now pose the question and ask what it was that Rosenzweig received from Schelling, the answer is "cosmic time,"

> a time whose three dimensions, present, past and future, are considered as the principle of God's creation of the world, a time lived by the religious man and independent of vulgar, astronomical or historical time. From this discovery Rosenzweig will see the problems from Schelling's perspective: mythology and revelation and from a new angle the relationship between Judaism and Christianity.[5]

If the relationship between Judaism and Christianity is now to be comprehended from Schelling's perspective, then the presentation of the problem is radically different from Cohen's ethical idealism and his decided rejection of Schelling's Identity-Philosophy, which he considered an aesthetic pantheism. "In this aesthetic meaning of pantheism lies a new danger for ethics and consequently, a proof of the relationship of the God concept to Ethics, and not to Logic and Metaphysics."[6] The issue between Cohen and Rosenzweig is clear. Everything depends upon the concept of time. The philosophy of Idealism is at issue.

Schelling in *The Ages of the World* makes the following comments on eternity:

> Metaphysicians, indeed, act as if there is a concept of eternity completely free of all admixture of concepts of time. They might be right if they speak of the eternity which is completely ineffectual toward all outside it, which is, as we have shown, like a nothing in relation to all else. From this kind of eternity the concept of the present, as well as that of the past and the future, is excluded. But as soon as they would talk about a real, living eternity, they do not know better than that this eternity is a continual 'now,' an eternal present.... True eternity is not that which excludes all time, but that which contains time (eternal time) subjected to itself.[7]

Like time, myth is an eternal truth that is continually re-creating itself. One of Schelling's most significant works was a philosophy of mythology. He was deeply concerned with divine life, with theogony. Deeply influenced by a work of the eighteenth-century traveler, essayist, novelist, and art connoisseur, Karl Philipp Moritz (1756-93), Schelling was particularly devoted to his work *Götterlehre* because as the title indicates it is concerned with theogony. Quoting Moritz we can grasp what are the fundamental perspectives of a philosophical mythology.

> In spite of the victory of the Olympians the older divinities remain still venerated, because they are opposed to the new divinities not as the corruptible and hateful is to the beneficent and the good, but as power rises up against power. Power is victorious over power and the conquered remain in their ruin still great. Under the empire of the Titans and the rule of Saturn, who devoured their own children, we still think the chaotic, the limitless, the crude ... yet we link again with this representation of the crude, the unbridled and limitless, which is subject to no compulsion, the concept of freedom and equality.... We place the golden age under dominance of Saturn.[8]

The chaotic is not only the first, but it is the ground of all reality. In the overcoming, *die Überwindung*, the chaotic is only driven into its ground; it is suppressed, *verdrungen*. The Titans remain alive; they are venerated. "Zeus *is* the conqueror of the monstrous, and this event, through which he realizes his essence, is manifested in the brightening of the Heavens."[9] The life of divinity like all life is dependent upon the ground, the chaotic. Without this ground there would be no realization of the divine essence. "Without the ground, *Grund*, the divine essence is not revealed. Its revelation is the overcoming of its opposite, which as what is overcome and opposed is its *ground*."[10] If we now ask where we are after having explored a moment of Schelling's speculative wanderings in mythology and their connections to Rosenzweig, we will have to dig somewhat deeper into Rosenzweig's speculations.

Fleischmann states that for Rosenzweig "the revolutionary act of Judaism is in the reversal of the temporal succession, a revolution going beyond even Nietzsche's imagination because with time everything is reversed, everything which is temporal."[11] Rosenzweig's remarks are significant:

> To live in time means to live between beginning and end. He who would live an eternal life, and not the temporal in time, must live outside of time, and he who would do this must deny that "between." But such a denial would have to be active if it is to result, not just in a not-living-in-time but in a positive living-eternally. And the active denial would occur only in the inversion. To invert a Between means to make its After a Before, its Before an After, the end a beginning, the beginning an end. And that is what the eternal people does.[12]

The Jewish people are eternal because they are the eternal "now" in which past, present, and future are not eliminated, but are alive in their eternal moments, living and re-creating themselves in the eternal "now." No moment is lost or denied, each is dependent upon the other, each lives from the other. They form an organic whole, alive in their mutuality and dependence. The life of the people is a microcosm of the divine life. In their eternity the people are divine. A divine people living among the other peoples of the world, but as they are alive in their history, the holy people are alive in their eternity. This people deny the "between," they refuse the omnipotence of temporality, they reject time as vulgar succession, but in eternity they embody the inversity of the Before and the After, the After and the Before.

The question that can be posed is whether *The Star of Redemption* is a Jewish book. "Rosenzweig's reply is significant because in spite of the non-Jewish character and non-traditional nature of his aims, his 'method' was entirely Jewish. The difference with Jewish thinkers of the XIX century is that Rosenzweig doesn't think about Judaism but thinks in Judaism."[13] In 1923 in "Der Jude" Rosenzweig published his essay "Apologetic Thinking" indicating that Jewish thought since the 1820s has remained apologetic, i.e., "thought remains dependent upon the provocation of opposition." "Thinking was not thinking about Judaism (which was simply taken for granted, and was more of an existence than an 'ism'); it was thinking within Judaism, learning—ultimately ornamental, rather than fundamental, thinking."[14] Beyond Apologetics, which never seems to fuse the thinker's essence with the essence of men, is ultimate knowledge. "Ultimate knowledge no longer defends; ultimate knowledge judges."[15] Apologetics belongs to temporality; it can become a defense of a part and not of the whole. Yet, it is not a defense in the usual sense of the word, it seeks the truth in its search for the essence of issues and men. At its greatest and most encompassing moment Apologetics never crosses over into judgment, it never stands in eternity. Remaining thought, it abides in time. The religious man exists in cosmic time, i.e., religious time. His life is the struggle against profane time. At its highest Apologetic thinking is profane.

From the perspective of Schelling's *Ages of the World* the eternity of time is inseparable from the eternity of *beginning*. "Here, too, it holds that the beginning must not know itself. This means it must not know itself as beginning. Nothing is or discerns itself at once as merely ground or beginning. Whatever is a beginning must regard itself not as a beginning but as essence (something which is not for its own sake) in order to be a true beginning."[16] Here we are standing within divine life perceiving a unity that is a becoming, "the eternal seed of God" which we can say is not yet God, the actual God, but only God's powers. God is in the state of possibility, for without this divine possibility there can be no birth of God into actuality. Rosenzweig speaks of God putting himself in the "need of redemption." The cosmic role of Israel is the unification of God, the unification that bears within itself Becoming.

> And this Becoming is enjoined on the souls and hands of man. Jewish man and Jewish law—nothing less than the process of redemption, embracing God, world, man, transpires between the two.... The "awe" with which the remnant (of Israel) turned itself into the dwelling-place of God, the "love" with which he thereupon proceeded to fulfill the law, he the individual, the "I" which fulfills the law.... The most constricted has expanded into the whole, the All.... The descent into the Innermost has disclosed itself as an ascent to the Highest.[17]

Eternal Israel belongs to divine life as redemptive truth, as the indwelling of God's love. In Israel, God's remnants are unified, the actuality of God is realized; but this is a realization that lies in negation, for in the process toward actuality there is a similar movement to irrationality. The eternity of Israel is the continuous internalization of a self whose nature drives it at the same time toward the world.

What, may we ask, is the difference between Judaism and Christianity? Rosenzweig believed that they both were expressions of God's truth: "Judaism lives at the end of cosmic time while Christianity lives at the beginning. For the Jew health is a perpetual past, for the Christian an eternal future."[18]

> Judaism and Christianity are two eternal dials for the week- and year-hand of time, time that is constantly being renewed. In them, in their year, the course of world-time, which cannot be imaged forth but only experienced and told, takes shape as an image . . . in Judaism it does not proceed from the Law, in Christianity it does not proceed from Faith: but in both, from the external, visible forms by whose means they wrest their eternity from time; in Judaism from the past of the Jewish people, in Christianity from the event on which the Christian community is founded, and only through these do Law and Faith become visible.[19]

To separate the profane from the holy, temporality from eternity, Rosenzweig speaks of a circle, the eternal movement of the religious calendar. In fact, we can speak of a philosophy embraced in the calendar year of holy events. Man is raised from his profane life by immersing himself in the calendar of holy events. The circular movement of the calendar is the eternal "now," from which and to which the past, present, and future flow. "With beginning, middle, and end, it can become what the mere sequence of individual and ever new moments never can: a circle returning upon itself."[20] The life of and in the holy calendar, its expression in prayer, realizes the divine, the eternal in man's life. The internalization of temporal reality transfigures and transforms finite existence into sacred reality. In the depths of the myth which creates the life of the holy calendar, in which the eternity of the people is expressed, there enters that mystical bond of blood from which it draws its immortality. Fleischmann comments that "in addition to this biological myth whose victim Rosenzweig becomes, there is also a 'folkloric' element. Rosenzweig thinks that the Jewish religion is essentially tied to Jewish popular life, which remained intact through history because of the uninterrupted transmission of popular tradition. . . . For this reason it appears that Judaism is the only religion where there is no break between the people and 'the image placed before his soul'; Judaism is characterized by the 'unity of myth.'"[21] The problems of the world become impure for the Jew and it is from this profane world that he escapes. He rejects the contradictions and relativities. From the secular calendar he moves to the religious one. Caught in the world of myth his life is a re-creation of holy events which give him his meaning and purpose. Having established a radical difference between the sacred and profane he feels himself close to truth and can with indifference reject all other life. As he moves closer and closer to the sacred he understands his life as universal and feels the universability of his deeds, his prayers, and his ritual. Covered in the prayer shawl of sanctity, all other life is devalued, the future is already in the past, the present the moment in which future and past become one. Incompleteness and the yet-to-be are notions which no longer have meaning. The believer "does not have to wait for world history to unroll its long course to let him gain what he feels he already possesses in the circuit of every year: the experience of the immediacy of each single individual to God, realized in the perfect community of all with God."[22] The reduction of political and moral responsibility to the realm of the profane negates the classical perception of man as a political being. We are faced with the dissolution of man as a physical and moral person. In fact, we have relegated these realms to the arbitrary, the consequence of political indifference. In this respect the political realm becomes the exclusive concern of arbitrary and tyrannical forms of power politics. How is it possible to live in political indifference and survive in the sacred calendar of eternal life? Here we are confronted with a dualism as severe, and perhaps more so, than that between the gods of light and darkness.

Rosenzweig was convinced that Judaism, being a reality in itself, needed no land and no state. "The Jewish people are obliged to live in dispersion because it is the destiny which is commensurate with their divine election. It is uniquely in the dispersion where they are most unhappy, isolated, and thrown upon themselves that they are most faithful to this vocation and to their fitting 'internal' nature."[23] "*Der Boden darf ihm nie Scholle werden.*" These words proclaim their difference from all the historical peoples. Their ground should never become their soil, a profound and agonizing separation between social and political values, and those that belong to eternity. Values are made to confront values and man who is body and soul is torn asunder.

Rosenzweig willingly admits that between Judaism and Christianity no judgment is possible because here we are faced with two lived experiences which can't be weighed and analyzed like two theories or two proofs. Yet, Rosenzweig does not allow the profane to have values which are lived with passion, hope, and respect; the very term "profane" already gives the victory to the sacred. The sacred becomes a sacred history, one generation transmits to the next a holy moment of the circular course of sacred history. "In the eternal people, procreation bears witness to eternity; on the eternal way this witness must really be attested to as witness. Every point of the way must once bear witness that it knows itself as midpoint of the eternal way. There the physical onward flow of the one blood bears witness to the ancestor in the engendered grandson."[24] Schelling conceived of history as the progressive divine revelation. In Rosenzweig's conception the eternal path of Judaism moves toward *Davids königlichen Spross*. Even in the circular movement there is a neverending revelation, a deepening consciousness of the divine reality, an ever-growing realization that time and eternity are one, that in every moment of time eternity exists. Each moment of time is an expression of eternity. Each moment of eternity reveals the rootedness of the eternal people. They are eternal in their eternity as eternity is the expression of the sacredness of their life. Here love and sacredness come together. Judaism reveals the ground of God's love to be in the communion of the people who in covenant overcome profane time and become an eternal people. Generations are linked together in holy communion, each separating the profane from the holy, each required to become aware again that Truth does not lie in a Beyond of life, but that this Truth is here and has been seen and heard. Each generation must learn how to see and how to hear. Each generation re-creates the myth of truth realizing and embodying itself in the process, knows the End is already in the Beginning and the self-creating process bears within itself the completeness of Beginning and End. When we think this grand myth which Rosenzweig has given us we wonder with astonishment at its imaginative powers. It is something toward which we feel drawn, in which we could find security and peace, but then we forget the world about us, its momentary and relative problems, and to that world we also belong. Nothing would do greater violence to our human existence if we abandoned the demands of "profane" time and space to become members of the eternal communion. Rosenzweig makes it possible for us to forget ethics, the comprehension of the pure will, the realization that meaning and purpose are our highest tasks, and that in an unfinished and incomplete world we discover the essence of our humanity. To this world Hermann Cohen addressed his philosophical System.

Speaking of our concern for the future, Karl Löwith in his book *Meaning in History* details the difference between the classical view of history and the Hebraic-Christian view of history as future. To illustrate this difference he poses two questions: How did it come about? How shall we go ahead? The first question is the classical; the second the biblical. To put the biblical in focus Löwith quotes Hermann Cohen, for whom the future submerges past and present:

> The concept of history is a product of prophetism. . . . What Greek intellectualism could not produce, prophetism has achieved. In Greek consciousness, *historein* is equivalent to inquiry, narration and knowledge. To the Greeks history remains something we can know because it is a matter of "fact" that is of the past. The prophet, however, is a seer, not a scholar; his prophetic vision has created our concept of history as being essentially future. . . . For this new future the "creator of heaven and earth" is not sufficient. He has to create "a new heaven and a new earth." In this transformation the idea of newness is implied. Instead of a golden age in the mythical past, the true historical existence on earth is constituted by an eschatological future.[25]

Ernst Cassirer has remarked that Cohen "of all modern thinkers has felt this fundamental idea of the Prophetic religion most deeply and renewed it in the greatest purity."[26] The concept of future must not be thought of as a time concept but as an ethical one. "Eternity is an ethical concept and as such it is related to the pure will and the moral self-consciousness."[27] If future as eternity is a moral concept, then it is a moral task which presupposes that what is real is not reasonable, but must become reasonable. The moral task affirms the unique role of the individual to be the source and beginning of responsibility and action. The world is not moral, but must become moral, and man is the source of this becoming. Cohen makes this clear: "In no way are we speaking of eternal time nor of an eternal place, but only of eternal work."[28] The reality of the moral consciousness is embodied in no goal nor in any concrete form which has historical identifiability; it belongs to moral action and this alone is eternal. Eternity, Cohen would say, is *ewige Aufgabe,* eternal task, the task of eternity, *die Aufgabe der Ewigkeit.*[29] Task and eternity become one. There is no temporal end to man's ethical task. Task means eternity. To think of an end of task is to think of man's demise. Task belongs to the eternity of the pure will. In fact, we can say with Cohen: "Eternity is its reality." This reality breaks the hold of myth. Truth is not in the past to be re-created and continually relived. It is the belief in a new beginning, "the beginning of a new time, a new world, a new mankind, i.e., a new mankind upon the earth."[30] This hope embraced Cohen's ethics. I believed that no hope or feeling was more powerful in Cohen's philosophy than this concept of future, the "new beginning." It permeated the Logic as well as the Aesthetic. We cannot conceive of a philosophy of history or a meaningful philosophy of politics without this orientation to the future. "The End of Days is the yet-to-come, toward which all political life strives, toward which all reality is orientated."[31] Messianism is an ethical ideal. The future is the magnetic center from which we begin to comprehend the past and the present. Neither can be grasped from themselves, from the future their meaning becomes comprehensible as past and present. The meaning of future depends upon man. No longer dominated and bound to the past or the present, he must give sense and purpose to them, and this is possible only if the future becomes the criterion of the Will.

Together with the concept of the future is that of the ideal. "In the struggle of existence there is no victory of eternity. Ethics builds the goal. The eternity of the moral self-consciousness, the eternity of mankind as the bearer of this self-consciousness—this is the ideal. It is the being of the Will; it is the highest being of Idealism."[32] We proceed from the Ideal if we want to comprehend the real. We begin with the future if we want to grasp the past. The future is anticipation, the source of movement and desire. "In thinking, eternity is an *Abstracktum,* the Will brings it to being, *Sein* . . . the being of the Ideal, i.e., the being of the pure Will."[33] The consequence of this pure idealization of time as future is the severe rejection of cosmogony and theogony. God is no longer at the beginning, at creation. He is at the end. God is no longer the origin of history; He is the goal and purpose of it. "Mankind did not live in any past and did not become alive in the present, only the future can bring about its bright and beautiful form. This form is an idea, not a shadowy image of the beyond."[34] Cohen was convinced that world history has just begun, the universal history of monotheism is at its beginnings. The truth of monotheism has yet to permeate man's history. World history begins with the end and makes the beginning comprehensible. On the 26 and 27 of May 1789 the poet Schiller gave his inaugural lecture on the meaning of world history, "Was heisst und zu welchem Ende studiert man Universalgeschichte?" In it Schiller makes the same point that Cohen does: "World history proceeds from a principle which is in contradiction to the Beginning. The real course of events descend from the origin of things to their most recent order, the universal historian goes from the most recent world situation to the origin of things."[35] World history must embody a teleological principle, a belief of reason, which is possible to give it meaning and purpose. Cohen in a rare moment of self-reflection speaks of his need to believe:

> For my own peace I need the confidence that hatred among people will be destroyed from the consciousness of mankind. ... All hatred is vain and wanton. All hatred is nothing but illusion, nothing but the interpretation and embellishment of human baseness ... if one recognizes in a more fundamental psychology, which is enlightened by ethics, that hatred is an illusory factor in the soul, then the greater part of the burden of sin falls from the human heart.[36]

Monotheism, world history, teleology belong to that philosophical commitment which knows the depths of the moral struggle in a world where peace is a religious and moral ideal. Cohen speaks the religious tradition when he refers to the "tent of peace." Peace transforms all life into a "feast." The experiences of history are no longer our guide, all is not known and events do not repeat themselves in a circular fashion. History does not embody the human experience. We are not the consequences of its teachings. The pessimism which it manifests in its continuous repetitions of conflicts, hatred, and power struggles is not the last word. Cohen refused to allow an analogy to exist between the historical life of man and the moral world. There is no doubt that the course of human events and the moral order do not coincide, but this lack of identity is the source and strength of moral belief and action. Here we discover the moral quality of man. The failure of the soul to drive from it those forces which attempt to destroy its purity of purpose and action is the pessimism which Cohen always believed threatened Idealism. Pessimism he believed was inspired by mysticism and exiled by rationalism. Hope is the foundation of Idealism, the belief in rationality, in the purity of the moral subject, in the feeling of humanity. Hope is inseparable from the future, from courage, trust, and peace.

Inseparable from the pure will is the consequent action which must follow from it. The ideal has social and political actions. Cohen speaks of the meaning of the Sabbath: "If Judaism had given only the Sabbath to the world, it would by this alone be identified as the messenger of joy and as the founder of peace among mankind. The Sabbath took the first step which led to the abolition of slavery, and the Sabbath also took the first step in showing the way to the abolition of the division of labor into manual and intellectual work."[37] If pessimism has a mystic origin, weakens the moral commitment, and paralyzes action, then sadness dilutes human feeling and loosens the tie with our fellow man. "The Jew," Cohen proclaims, "cannot remain a man of sorrow." We could easily repeat the sentence and say that the philosopher of Idealism cannot remain a "man of sorrow." We are moved and commanded by the goal, by the future. We know and believe in the eternity of the task. Monotheism proclaiming the uniqueness of God, *die Einzigkeit Gottes,* has only begun to be realized in mankind. We live in conflict. What we see about us is the world of Hobbes. In contradiction to this Hobbesian reality, begins the struggle for universality, the refusal of eudaemonianism, national self-interest, and hate. The ethics of Cohen reach their most concrete moment when he actualizes the contradiction between historical materialism and idealism in the idea of "the pious of the peoples of the world." In this community of men embracing all religions and men of good will there is alive that belief in monotheism, that ideal of humanity that makes it possible for them to be watchmen and fighters for rationalism of Idealism.

When we think of Cohen and Rosenzweig we are confronted with two diametrically opposed world-views. Time for Cohen was only future. "The primeval past is as little ideal as the beyond of the afterworld. The latter, too, is merely the continuation of the past and the present, but not the newness of the future. This newness consists in the dawning of the ideal in contrast to all actuality. Myth is everywhere the sunrise of culture, but the sunny day of morality does not yet dawn within it."[38] Cohen rejected Schelling because of his Identity-Philosophy, because he reduced divinity to the process of mythology, and above all because he wrote no particular Ethics, "keine besondere Ethik geschrieben hat." No more damaging criticism could come from his pen. It is hard to imagine what Cohen would have thought of Rosenzweig's *Star of Redemption*. We can only assume that he would have found it difficult to comprehend. He would be uncomfortable with the influence which Schelling exercised, and would perhaps have thought it more prudent to be moved by the *Critique of Practical Reason* than the *Ages of the World* and the *Philosophy of Mythology*. The deep gap separating the future from the past and the present brought forth the prophet in Cohen. He felt the depths of the moral self in the struggle against the moment and its moral and political inadequacy and indifference, but he knew and believed in the need to confront, challenge, and act against it. No such radical separation between the holy and the profane would have been endurable for Cohen. Thus, separation was a moral problem, a moral task and responsibility, not given and indestructible realities existing from eternity. Cosmic time defies the newness of the future, it is self-enclosed time. The future is the radically other, the new earth and the heavens. Over and over again we hear these words of Cohen: "Mankind did not live in any past and did not become alive in any present."[39] The moral act is a challenge to every man who knows the need to break into universality, to break away from the experiences of history, and who knows that history as world history begins with the Future. "The creator of heaven and earth is not sufficient for this being of the future. He must create 'a new heaven and a new earth.'" The future stands in opposition to all that was and is. The future is diametrically opposed to all myths—those of the past, those of the present, and those yet to come.

Yet, it is the future which makes the philosophy of history a possibility. The future is the guide for those who seek meaning and purpose, for those who not only think, but act, who not only know, but believe, and who grasp the belief of reason as the essence of philosophical dialogue. Monotheism and the future are one. "Tolerance is a principle that cannot be valid for the origin, setting up, and establishing of monotheism. With regard to this question there can be no oscillating or any mutually conditioned and restrictive recognitions of opposites: the being or nonbeing of the moral universe is at stake here."[40] The moral universe is at stake for Cohen with the defeat or victory of monotheism. For those who are committed, there is indeed no oscillation. Belief involves one's moral being, it demands action and decision. The belief in reason outlaws those ideologies and thoughts which imply its destruction. Both Cohen and Rosenzweig were believers, but their concepts of time made it possible for each to comprehend the future and history in diametrically different ways.

4

The Conflict with Myth and Evil

In 1904 Hermann Cohen completed his *Ethics of the Pure Will*, a magisterial text the likes of which has not been seen since Kant had written his *Critique of Practical Reason* (1788). For all its majesty this text of over 600 pages has been rarely read and detailedly commented upon by philosophers. Steven Schwarzschild, who wrote the introduction to a reissued text, opted to allow his introductory essay to remain in English. He made the following comment on this decision:

> This introduction to the German text has been kept in the English language form in which it was written, though the author could have reverted to the language of his childhood. H. Cohen's philosophy and Marburg neo-Kantianism in general have, after all, suffered the tragically paradoxical fate that German-language culture, out of whose spirit and toward which they were largely oriented, rejected them virtually from their inception and, through the decades, with cataclysmically exponentialized vehemence for not being "authentically German," and in non-German-language cultures, on the other hand, they never had a fair chance in the first place for, among other things, being "too German."[2]

The task is now to consider the problems which distinguish Cohen's *Ethics* and give it its unique place in the history of philosophy. I believe that we can deal with the text if we choose particular problems and discuss their development in Kant and Cohen. The problems of evil and mythology are at the center of Cohen's concern, and his attitude toward them makes it possible to find meaningful his belief in the purity of the self, efficacy of the future, faith in law, and the acceptance of God as the principle of truth. I propose to deal with these problems beginning with Kant's *Religion within the Limits of Reason Alone,* his "On the Failure of All Attempted Philosophical Theodicies," F. W. J. Schelling's *Of Human Freedom,* and Cohen's *Ethics of the Pure Will* and *Religion of Reason.* The task is to discover the uniqueness of Cohen's position, what the implications of it are, and from what sources it arises.

Cohen declares univocally that "there is no evil. Evil is only a concept that is derived from that of freedom. In myth alone is there a power of evil. It is the dominance of myth which in theology and metaphysics advances a diabolical divine power.... The victory of the good means the preservation of the good against the doubts, hesitations, and experiences which bear upon the natural and historical incompleteness of the human condition."[3] This clear and precise declaration by Cohen is not limited to a particular text, but wherever and whenever the problem of evil and human nature arise Cohen maintains this position. He never wanes in his belief and conviction that man is morally responsible for what he does and that before God and his fellow man this responsibility remains unchallenged. Nothing blights the human condition more deeply than cultural pessimism and the intellectual and moral refusal to affirm the goodness of man and the ideal of his perfectibility. Cohen's optimism belongs to his respect for the future; it is a philosophical faith in the ever-deepening self-consciousness of the pure will. Before we can comprehend Cohen's philosophical and religious commitments, we should place them against the background of the Kant he venerated and the Schelling whose philosophy of mythology he suspected and whose concept of human freedom he denied.

The philosopher Eric Weil was of the opinion that Kant spoke of radical evil not to devalue man but to make it possible for him to become more human.[4] It would seem that the Kant texts bear out this judgment. Keenly observant of human nature, Kant saw clearly man's "unsocial sociability." He explained it by saying that men have "a tendency to come together in society, coupled, however, with a continual resistance which threatens to break this society up. This tendency is obviously rooted in human nature."[5] Man's refusal to dominate his egoism, to reduce all values to private ambitions and desires, can be called evil. "Genuine evil consists in this, that man does not will to withstand these inclinations when they attempt to transgress . . . so it is really this disposition that is the true enemy."⁶ Man's moral development is at its beginning. We are aware that the moral command which enunciates that we *ought to be* better human beings is not necessarily commensurate with our ability to be better men. Kant believed that "we cannot start from an innocence natural to us but must begin with the assumption of a wickedness of the will in adapting its maxims contrary to the original moral disposition; and since this propensity to evil is inextirpable we must begin with the incessant counteraction against it."⁷ The counteraction lies in human freedom, in the depths of man's awareness of his moral fallibility, but it is counteraction which offers little assurance of success. Man can *hope,* he can believe in the efficacy of his own actions; but he is aware that the efforts are endless and success only a hope. Yet this self-awareness of the conflict in us is already the beginning of our moral recovery. Whatever the consequences of the struggle, what is of greatest significance is that we are responsible for the task, which is to make us better men. It is essential to know that *man himself* is accountable for the propensity of evil, "which, as it affects the morality of the subject, is to be found in him as a free-acting being and for which it must be possible to hold him accountable as the offender."⁸ Nothing is more fundamental to Kant's outlook on man's nature than his realization that when man substituted the private sense, *sensus privatus,* for the common sense, *sensus communis,* he became socially unsocial. Hope and belief make it possible to affirm that it is possible to bring goodness from evil, that it is possible to educate man to the good, and that the moral education of man is a collective responsibility. Kant had noticed "that when any other animal species is left to its own devices, each individual attains its complete destiny but in man's case only the species, at most, achieves it."⁹

Radical evil is the decision made for the private sense, for self-love; it is not a decision for evil, but the attempt to reduce all value to personal interest. Kant's observations became the foundation for a philosophy of history and religion. He proclaimed the teachings of Christ to be revolutionary. Human history and morality do not coincide; but the realization of the struggle to overcome the reduction of life to self-love is the ground of freedom. Admitting that man has a propensity for evil, we are nevertheless forced to hold him responsible for it, "we can further call it a radical, innate evil in human nature yet none the less brought upon us by ourselves."[10] Reflecting on this self which must and therefore can dominate the evil propensity, Kant interprets the biblical text of Job. Here we have a figure who has interested and fascinated man's moral, poetical, and religious imagination. Job is afflicted by God, yet he knows he had not consciously sinned against Him. If he sinned without knowing, then his sins are forgiven. Job's sufferings are, however, great. He is deprived of his wealth, authority, friends, and family. His good conscience was alone left to him. Without it Job would have had no possibility for moral questions, doubts, and struggle. "The friends of Job accepted the doctrine which explains all woes in the world by reference to divine Justice; they are punishments for crimes committed."[11] Job was conscious of a simple fact: he had human frailties; his conscience did not accuse him; God created him a limited and dependent being. "Job spoke as he thought, as he felt, and as every man in his position would feel. His friends, however, spoke as if they were overheard by the Almighty whose behavior they were judging, and as if they cared more for winning his favors by passing the right judgments than for saying the truth."[12] Job accuses his friends of dishonesty, of attempting to explain divinity when they should have admitted their doubts and lack of knowledge. It is this rare honesty which is lacking in mankind. Man is not seduced from without; he is seduced from within. Man's hypocrisy is his seducer. Man must know the limits of his knowledge. Man is seduced when he wants to know the relationship between divine justice and human action. Our comprehension begins after the fact; we learn from what has occurred. In our lack of knowledge we begin to understand that we must be responsible for meaning and action. In the recognition of the limitations of our knowledge begins the possibility of "negative wisdom." "We can understand the necessary limits of our reflections on the subjects which are beyond our reach."[13] This was Job's wisdom. Job preferred to comprehend what he didn't and couldn't comprehend. He did know that the faith which arose from the "conviction of his ignorance" allowed him to root this faith in moral conviction. Job's resolve to be sincere is inseparable from his conviction that truth is beyond his and all knowledge. Truth is in his confession that it is beyond him." One cannot guarantee that everything one says to one's self or to others is *true* (for one can err), but one can and must always guarantee that what one says is *sincere* for of this everyone can be immediately certain."[14] So convinced of this was Kant that he concludes his reflections on Job with some clear and incisive remarks on lying, which he always considered to be the arch destroyer and seducer of morality.

> He who says to himself (or to God; in matters of religion this amounts to the same thing) that he *believes* something, without having perhaps given a single look at himself to ascertain whether he is indeed certain... of his conviction tells a *lie,* and his lie is not only the most stupid one before the One who searches the heart, but it is also the most criminal one because it cuts under the ground of sincerity, the bases of every virtue.[15]

Having no illusions of the goodness of his fellow man, Kant believed that it was not necessary to travel the earth to confirm this view. There was no distinction between the cities and hamlets. People did not improve as a consequence of geography nor grow worse in the luxuries of the cities. The "inclination to lie" corrupted man everywhere. It reduced man to "worthlessness, an evil which completely ruins the character of the man."[16] Look in to your own breast, Kant tells us, in it you find the seducer. Kant doesn't seek the origin of evil in suprasensible reality, nor does he ascribe it to fate and necessity. Man's moral life is a confrontation which each human, who allows himself to consider and take seriously the moral problem, becomes aware of as soon as he realizes that there is a difference between what he wants to do and what he does. We are easily persuaded that the seduction of lying can be ascribed to forces beyond ourselves, but what we need to be aware of is that we are free and responsible and in this lies the possibility of our moral strength and capacity. However corrupt or seduced we may be, we are never devoid of choice and decision. Cohen was certain that the concern must be centered on the moral self. He felt it to be a serious misconception to focus interest on the origin of evil. "Where interest adheres primarily to the origin of evil we can suppose that ethics is no longer the principle thought."[17] Here we become engaged in myth, in cultural pessimism and the consequential political and moral decay. In this respect Cohen reflected the danger which he observed in the *Kulturpessimismus* movement, "its emphasis on instinct and intuition, blind forces beyond the reach of the concept and prior to the understanding and all discursive thought. . . . Truth is found in the irrational impulses of our inner life, and beyond that are only the lucubrations of scientists and rationalists."[18] We should be aware that the comprehension of Cohen demands not only a knowledge of the philosophical tradition, but a historical understanding of the irrational forces and their literary activity in Germany before the First World War.

Cohen's judgments on the philosopher Schelling refer to the fact that he ascribed to myth truth. In it we can discover the meaning of divine life and revelation. Schelling identified the problem of freedom with that of evil.[19] If we would say that Cohen had particular forces and traditions which he wanted to overcome, then we would say that they were embodied in the philosophy of Schelling. Here we find explorations in the nature of divine life, an assumption precious to mythology and Gnosticism. In Schelling's *Philosophische Untersuchungen über das Wesen der menschliche Freiheit und die damit zusammenhangenden Gegenstände*[20] we are led into the labyrinth of Schelling's speculations. These speculations are based on the assumption that life is an attribute of God. Schelling's philosophy is a journey into that life. Philosophy and theogony are the same. If we assume that *Gott ein Leben ist, nicht bloss ein Sein,* then evil has ontological existence.

> All life has a destiny and is subject to suffering and development. God freely submitted Himself to this too, in the very beginning, when in order to become personal He divided light and the world of darkness. For being is only aware of itself in becoming. . . . All history remains incomprehensible without the concept of a humanly suffering God, a concept which is common to all the mysteries and spiritual religions of ancient times.[21]

Within this divine process we reflect the life process of man. Opposing and consuming wills abide in us; they parallel the ancient theogonies. They struggle with each other but do not completely and immediately overcome each other. "If it were conquered sooner, the good would remain concealed in it together with the evil."[22] In the "depths" these opposing forces only increased in intensity preparing for their separation. Divinity is not yet "all in all," is not yet realized. Good and evil are

Myth and Evil   63

still together in the "depths." In the "will of the deep" is the ground of particularization; divinity is the source of universalization. The anxiety of life and the consuming power which burns in the will of particularity is the "will of the deep," similar to that will of love which is unconquerable and yet has not the force nor the will to dominate the "will of the deep." Each will must live independently of the other, neither one conquers the other or is conquered by it. Man stands before these two forces and must choose. The choice for good or evil is not one which puts the other to rest or has the possibility to deprive it of its actuality. The force to willfulness and the force to live remain ever-confronting forces. The "will of the deep" and the will of love expound the theogony, the life of the godhead, where these two forces belong to each other and exist alongside each other giving life to divinity, a life which analogously is man's. Man, neither, can be love nor chaos; whichever force he is inclined toward only suppresses its "other"; it strengthens it in its suppression. This "other" lives and can break forth whenever and wherever. Man is the eruptive center of these forces, which are more powerful than man, and in which man comes to know himself; he is because these forces are. Schelling concluded his remarks with this observation:

> In this system there is one principle for everything; it is one and the same being reigning in the dark depths of nature and eternal clarity, one and the same effecting the severity and isolation of things, and unity and kindness, the same thing that rules with the will of love in goodness and wills the will of anger in evil. ... Evil, however, is no being but a counterfeit of being which is real only by contrast, not in itself. Moreover absolute identity, the spirit of love, is prior to evil, just because the latter can only appear in contrast to it.[23]

If we think of Zeus controlling the forces of chaos, i.e., the children of Gaia and Uranus, and if we understand that this controlling force only suppresses but does not eliminate them, then we can comprehend Schelling's contrasting forces needing each other to be each other.

This identification of philosophy and mythology became the fate of Schelling's philosophical development. Embodied in his philosophical theogony, ethics is lost in the divine life. Cohen was eager to adhere to

Maimuni's separation of the attribute of life from the idea of God. "Thus, the Middle Ages continued in true religiosity the fundamental thought that God is an idea." Every attempt to identify God with person and with life distorts the relationship between God and man. The attempt to reduce man to a microcosm of theogonic life is to deprive him of that moral responsibility which is possible only where the difference between man and God makes it necessary for man to be responsible for the realization of the concept of humanity. Consequently, "the true definition of the relationship of God with man is not identification, but approachability (*Annährung*) through the eternal achievement of moral duty without which human life would have no meaning and man would become an animal."[24] Every attempt to make the life of God a source for imitation identifies divinity and humanity, God and nature, and commits the inevitable consequence of pantheism. God was for Cohen the incomparable, the unique, the inimitable. "God can't be considered as the 'example' of moral achievement; He is the eternal ideal of morality, the sufficient reason of all moral action, the supreme moral law and the only name adequate for Him is the 'source of morality,' *Urbild der Sittlichkeit*."[25] Seeking an example of that rare quality of honesty, the purity of intentions, Kant reflected upon the example of Spinoza. In the *Critique of Judgment* Kant spoke of Spinoza as that "righteous man . . . who considers himself firmly persuaded that there is no God and—since in respect of the object of morality a similar result ensues—no future life either."[26] But Kant questioned whether it was possbile for this righteous man to find a realization of his worthiness subject to the natural conditions which engulf man and beast. "Thus the end which this rightminded man would have, and ought to have, in view of the pursuit of the moral law would certainly have to be abandoned as impossible."[27] To remain faithful to the moral law, to the purity of intentions, i.e., to the purity of self, he must assume a "moral author of the world." "As this assumption at least involves nothing intrinsically self-contradictory he may quite readily make it from a practical point of view, that is to say, at least for the purpose of framing a conception of the possibility of the final end morally prescribed to him."[28] The confindence which we put into the moral law corresponds to the efficacy and significance of the premise which it embodies. The idea of God makes it possible to realize that confidence which we need to attain the capacity to assume the law as a moral duty. The purity of self requires the idea of God as the inimitable source of moral obligation. It is an idea that has its foundation in our reason and which profoundly satisfies the need and goal of reason. Righteousness alone without the idea of God fails to give purpose and sense to human history and existence; it allows this history and existence to be reduced to the natural consequences of moral indifference. God is the source of the philosophy of history.

Kant had spoken of Job's "free and sincere outspokenness," of the hypocrisy of Job's friends, of Job's refusal to flatter even God. He admired Job for his fearlessness; he spoke of Job's honesty as his refusal to lie, his domination of that "foul taint" which corrupts human life. Job was rewarded; God "honored Job by showing him the wisdom of His creation and its unfathomable nature."[29] Job becomes the moral teacher, one of the revolutionaries in history who remind us by their lives that the purity of intention is efficacious and eternal. "Yet the good principle has descended in mysterious fashion from heaven into humanity, not at one particular time alone, but from the first beginnings of the human race, and it rightfully has in mankind its first dwelling place."[30] Jesus is another revolutionary example of this indwelling of the purity of self. Kant's emphasis is upon the good works, the revolutionary nature and quality of this moral example. Examples are guides, they do not commend arbitrarily. Divinity remains the unique, inimitable, and incomparable idea, never to be realized but only approaching. Nothing could be more destructive to man's effort than the possibility that a divine grace assists him in his moral efforts; a heteronomous principle would destroy human responsibility and action. There is no God for those who abandon their fate and who "prefer moral servitude." This servitude gives lie to human existence, it fixes the divine appearance to a particular and distinct historical past event and allows the particular moment to be embraced and embodied in dogma. The faith of the philosopher which satisfies and promotes reason can only affirm the principle of a "universal religion of reason" which one day will supplant the ecclesiastical faith and domination which is the rule of all historical religions born in distinct moments of revelation. "Such, therefore, is the activity of the good principle, unnoted by human eyes but ever continuing—erecting for itself in the human race, regarded as a commonwealth under laws of virtue, a power and kingdom which sustains the victory over evil and under its own domination, assures the world of eternal peace."[31] The victory over evil was never doubted by Kant, and perhaps the moral faith achieved a profundity and strength only in the comprehension of man's evil inclination and the degree to which he allows it to develop both individually and collectively. The philosopher belongs to that revolutionary spirit and action which challenge the inclination to distortion, violence, and hypocrisy in human history. The philosopher more than others is aware of the gulf that separates the ethics of the pure will from the course of human events, but it is in this gulf that the decision for the ethical is made and the strength for its realizations developed. If the "Teacher of the Gospel" is a revolutionary, then it is only because he refuses the servitude that puts one man under the tutelage of another, that allows one man or institution to think for another. A religious leader or teacher is revolutionary if he proclaims the import and sense of the *aude sapere,* the dare to know. There can be no ethical action without knowledge, no love of God without love of learning. Kant did not spare Christianity the poor consequences of its historical life. "At any rate, the history of Christendom, from the time that it became a learned public itself, or at least part of the universal learned public, has served in no way to recommend it on the score of the beneficent effect which can justly be expected of a moral religion."[32] If we put it harshly, the history of religions contradicts the ethical intentions of their projected visions. With Hermann Cohen we have some solace: he believed that the history of Monotheism was only in its beginnings. The belief that God was the principle of truth was rooted in a confidence which made any dwelling upon evil unsuitable and incommensurate with his messianic hope.

Cohen remarked that the value of the Book of Job lies in its rejection of the relationship between sin and suffering and that suffering must be comprehended within the theodic concept of a moral world.[33] With Cohen's deep belief in the emergence of monotheism and its ethical consequence the notion of suffering takes on cosmic proportion. "Suffering is a true form of prophecy" because the proclamation of God's demand has not yet the potency to create that correlation between man and God in which the purity of moral subject is realized and can become efficacious. The future belongs to this correlationship and it is to this future, and the hopes and visions that it embodies, that the "sufferings of love" become manifest and acute. The formulae of Job's friends who affirmed the balance between sin and punishment had to be set aside. Job was aware that he suffered undeservedly, that there was no justification for the punishment which followed from the sins which he believed he didn't commit. The sufferings could only be those of love, those that would follow from the affirmation of the oneness and majesty of God. They are the sufferings of prophecy, in no way distinct from those which are endured by those whose commitment is the moral law and its demands.

In a 1915 publication, *The Concept of Religion in the System of Philosophy*, a book which he dedicated to the Marburg School, Cohen commented on a chapter of Isaiah. "The 53 Chapter of Isaiah is perhaps the greatest wonder of the Old Testament."[34] Cohen called it a parable and asked if it has a solution or if it must remain forever unrresolved. The parable begins with a new message: "Who hath believed our report ... surely he hath borne our griefs and carried our sorrows ... he was wounded for our transgressions, he was bruised for our iniquities: the chastisement of our peace was upon him."[35] Cohen calls him a prophet of heroism, the servant of God reaching the heights of martyrdom. Differing from Paul and the Christology of the Middle Ages, Cohen says that "in this chapter nothing recalls the thought that God's justified punishment should be satisfied through this representative atonement. Not for the atonement, the satisfaction of the divine judge is the suffering of a representation, but rather only for man to whom the suffering belongs, from whom it was taken by God's servant."[36] Suffering is not the consequence of sin or the punishment for it, but "suffering is the supreme moment of human power and worth."[37] Cohen continues his quotation: "for he was cut off out of the land of the living. The marvel belongs not only to his own age, but to all history." Cohen's concluding words reflect his conviction that the love of God is suffering. Yet it is not a suffering without joy and peace. "The pious suffer and not by chance, but according to a divine plan that he become the representative of mankind opposed to the corrupt and distorted world."[38] If God's suffering servant is the representative of mankind, dare we not say that Cohen believed as deeply in the uniqueness and truth of philosophical idealism as he did in the symbol of the suffering servant. They both have their source in the idea of God. We can agree with Eugène Fleischmann when he states that Cohen "admitted no dualism or contradiction between his philosophical work and his ideas on Judaism."[39] Cohen could believe that "the suffering hero Job represents the ideal of mankind" because his honesty was his refusal to reduce religious and moral life to the equation of sin and punishment, an old form of materialism. The "sufferings of love" belong to the idea of God as the incomparable other, incomparable to any living being. This uniqueness is the very essence of monotheism, whose reality makes all others form only possibilities. Evil lies in the fact that possibility assumes the right to claim totality. Evil gives lie to the nature of existence; it is its falsification.

As we mentioned, Schelling's thoughts on human freedom and evil present us with ideas that Cohen found unacceptable from a methodological and ethical perspective. To make the issue even clearer let us state a few of the fundamentals of Schelling's philosophy of mythology. Myth has its own necessity and therefore is "in accordance with the idealist concept of the object, its own *reality*."[40] The process by which God becomes conscious of Himself moving from abstraction to polytheism and to conscious unity is paralleled in human consciousness. There is a necessitating process of awareness embodying and preserving all the moments of the development; the truth of the end is the realization of the steps through which the end is achieved. Mythology embraces and determines human reality. "It is not by its history that the mythology of a nation is determined but, conversely, its history is determined by its mythology—or rather, the mythology of a people does not *determine* but *is* its fate, its destiny as decreed from the very beginning."[41] The mythological process embodies a truth which it is continually re-creating; it absorbs within itself every element of what we would consider the private sphere of life. The human and divine are merged, the contingent and the necessary become the same; a ritual dominates every aspect of life, and every stage has its own ceremonial character and quality. Against this organic whole any attempt to assert a nonritualistic attitude becomes a lese majesty and is punishable. Words like *Volk, Führer,* organism, blood, land, history are endowed with sacred and ceremonious qualities. The relationship between man and God is no longer rational, satisfying knowledge and ethics. It is an embodiment of God's life and the process which this life delineates. Man, like God, passes through moments of alienation and reconciliation allowing each to rise from relativity, differentiation, alienation to the absolute One. No moment of concrete existence is saved from the theogonic process. This ultimate unity absorbs into itself every moment of particularization. In fact, we observe a development in which the particular loses its status as a true form of reality and in losing its recognized being fades away into the Whole. Whatever ethics may be in this philosophy of mythology, it has become inseparable from the identity-philosophy which reveals itself as pantheism. Ethics loses its autonomy, man his responsbility and capacity for choice.

Cohen saw in pantheism the assimilation of the individual to the divine. He bore in himself a deep respect for the individual, for the moral autonomy of will, for the joy that arose in the search for knowledge, and for the idea that time was only future. Nothing reveals this more deeply than an article which Cohen published in *Der Jude* during World War I in which he related the experiences of a trip he made to Eastern Europe. He wanted to make this trip to speak of an idea which was of vital imprtance to him. "My plan is to vitalize in these countries the foundation of a free, energetic religiosity in keeping with their cultural capabilities and to work toward the establishment of seminaries for the Science of Judaism. A true life of religiosity for a cultured man is contingent on the living connection with religious science and religious education."[42] Cohen spoke of the "idealism of deep-rooted endurance" that he found in the Jews he visited, their "indestructible sense of life and world inherent in these still-natural people."[43] I cite this article, which is autobiographical, because it illustrates what theory only elaborates. Cohen's life commitment embraced not only the seminar hall, the publication of books, but a profound concern for human suffering and need. Cohen cared about those whose lives could be helped, and it was not beyond the dignity of the distinguished professor of Marburg to extend a helping hand. The realization of the *Ethics of the Pure Will* is in the deed; Cohen not only stated this but embraced it in action

The final chapter of Cohen's *Ethics* is concerned with humanity. "Humanity alone realizes the state, raises it beyond the atavism of the race instinct which is perhaps rooted in sexual perversity."[44] Humanity embodies those forces of human feeling which revolt against every attempt to elicit from the individual the elemental destructive powers which return him to a state of nature, which cause him to glorify the race and the soil, the leader, and the myth of sacred origins. Cassirer at the end of his book *The Myth of the State* (1945), prudently comments that "it is beyond the power of philosophy to destroy the political myths. A myth is in a sense invulnerable. It it impervious to rational arguments. ... When we first heard of the political myths we found them so absurd and incongruous, so fantastic and ludicrous that we could hardly be prevailed upon to take them seriously. By now it has become clear to all of us that this was a great mistake."[45] Cohen's fears of atavism reflect an awareness of a literature which could only have caused him deep pain and disquiet: W. H. Riehl's works in *Volkskultur,* Paul de Lagarde's *German Writings* (1878), and Julius Langbehn's *Rembrandt the Educator* (1890). "Better to split wood," Lagarde cried, "than to continue this contemptible life of civilization and education: we must return to the sources [of our existence], on lovely mountain peaks, where we are ancestors, not heirs."[46] Langbehn appealed directly to the "uncorrupted, un-miseducated and uninhibited youth . . . to raise the *Volksthum* to restore the organic community, which would lead to a resurgence of individuality and a rebirth of art and a truly German culture."[47] All this Cohen called *Atavismus der Rasseninstinkte.* Clearly he observed that "the natural element of the people easily infects patriotism with stains, the poison of national vanity, which degenerates into hate and jealousy. This naturalism which is now designated as nationalism is the strongest enemy of all those social and spiritual forces upon which depend the sincerity and activity of the state's progress."[48] With all the fine distinctions Cohen makes between humanity, humaneness, and mankind, one important consequence arises and that is that humanity points to the individual and refuses to allow the particular person to be lost to a general concept. Humanity, Cohen finally tells us, is parallel to the Greek word *sophrosyne.* It is the "virtue of character." The term must be explained with multiple sentences. "It is the unity of the spiritual-moral being. It is moderation to be understood only if we think of what the word measure, *mesor,* had in the Greek language. It is self-domination, a dominance by which the self becomes throne and empire."[49] The word was precious for Cohen because in it the circle of philosophical speculation had achieved its fulfillment. Humanity looked in all directions and had no fear to turn backwards. Humanity could now be identified with critical philosophy; "humanity has, in virtue of its full circumference, entered into the System of Philosophy."[50] In fact, we can say it is the expression of the System; it is the "virtue of *human feeling,*" the cultivation of that sense of humaneness which made it possible for Cohen to write his *Ethics* and to embody it in his communal activities. We have seen from his descriptions of his travels to the Jewish communities in Poland in 1914 and the efforts which he made to aid the Jews of eastern Europe that his sense of community was active and participatory. "Feeling is everything." The pure will has its final support in humanity as the virtue of human feeling, *Tugend der Menschengefühls*.

Cohen's veneration of Kant follows from the commitment both philosophers made to ethics as the central problem of philosophy. Clear is Cohen's rejection of any philosophical speculation which reduced the role of the individual as a moral being. Cohen in his *Religion of Reason* stated that "the discovery of the individual through sin is the source to which all religion returns. This knowledge is thought of as self-knowledge. Thus is religion to be distinguished from mythology in which man is not the cause of his sin, but rather the heir of his ancestor and his guilt."[51] The redemption from sin is every man's responsibility. Sin is a personal act for which each man is responsible. It has no cosmic reality and no ontological status. No attempt to make evil a force over which man has no control can promote man's moral life. If man is reduced to a marionette whose strings are pulled and manipulated by powers beyond him, then ethics is reduced to a logic whose premises belong to transcendent powers in which man is absorbed and finally eliminated as a moral subject. Cohen ended his *Ethics* with Humanity. He concluded his *Religion of Reason* with Peace. If each book is read in reverse, as every worthwhile book should be read, then we can comprehend Cohen's system as the expression of humanity: pure reason, pure will, pure feeling. Peace and joy are the expressions of our devotion to the oneness and uniqueness of God, making it possible to think of the growing unity of creation. Before God the law proclaims justice, courage, truthfulness, and trust. The mission of monotheism and its proclamation in the Torah gave Cohen a joy which he said was incomparable in its depths and feeling. "What are all the sacrifices in relationship to this historical mission, what are all the material and spiritual sufferings to this pure joy of knowledge and search! The joy in the Torah is the peace of the soul, the feasts of satisfaction."[52] If we begin the reading of the *Religion of Reason* with this feeling of mission and joy, we would have found requirements for the penetration of its spirit, for Humanity which is Monotheism. Two evils appear to threaten this joy; they are hate and pessimism. "Hate is always a groundless hate, *ein grundloser Hass*."[53] Cohen was certain that people only convince themselves that they hate each other. Regarding pessimism he says:

"We don't believe in pessimism, we disdain its wisdom because we have conceived more deeply and correctly the meaning of the world."[54] Citing these statements at the end of the article makes them meaningful; they embody a depth of thinking and believing, an understanding of an age latent with destructive forces which were later to destroy civilizations. Cohen might declare with prophetic simplicity and directness that "all hate is in vain," but philosophy doesn't rule history, nor does it change the attitude of those for whom philosophy is a mockery. Eric Weil, a student of Cassirer, often repeated the statement that man didn't have to think. To be concerned with philosophy is not natural, it requires "a decision which few of us make. The search for universality and universability of the ethical belongs to the calling of philosophy. The philosopher needs to believe, he knows the efficacy of belief, and what he believes reveals the nature of his calling. Cohen said: "Messianism links mankind with every individual being. For my own peace I need the assurance that hatred among peoples, *Völkerhass,* will be extinguished from mankind's culture consciousness, *Kulturbewusstsein der Menschheit.*"[55] Through all the difficult technicalities of his System, clear and precise thoughts speak powerfully and meaningfully to every being who is prepared to read them. Cohen submerges past and present in the future; he stood forth in forceful opposition to the sacredness of origins so dear to myths. The future is the purest idealization of time; it is the unity of Cohen's Idealism. "The future is the reality of history, *Die Zukunft wird die Wirklichkeit der Geschichte.*"[56] With these words Cohen showed us the direction and force of his philosophy. No thinker before him had been so deeply dedicated to time as future, as the ethical and moral demand, as the promise of the Messianic Kingdom.

5

The Despair of Ressentiment and the Power of Compassion

For every human phenomenon there corresponds an age in which it is distinctly comprehended and appreciated. Ressentiment had long been recognized but easily placed among other emotive phenomena and lost sight of in comparisons and quickly devised explanations and definitions. The phenomenon awaits its time to reveal its uniqueness and depths with which it penetrates the human mind. In 1915, the philosopher Max Scheler published his first version of his study of ressentiment: *Das Ressentiment im Aufbau des Moralen*.[1] There he defined ressentiment as "a self-poisoning of the mind which has quite definite causes and consequences. It is a lasting mental attitude, caused by the systematic repression of certain emotions and effects which, as such, are normal components of human nature. Their repression leads to the constant tendency to indulge in certain kinds of value delusions and corresponding value judgments. The emotions and affects primarily concerned are revenge, hatred, malice, envy, the impulse to detract and spite."[2] We face the problem of the meaning of these value illusions and delusions, the judgments which emerge from them, and what is most dangerous, the realization that the repression of these emotional feelings intensify and deepen their evocative powers. This can be understood through the increasing aggression which intensifies in repression. What Scheler has pointed to is the peculiar human condition which develops in states of social, political and economic inequality. This condition is ressentiment. It is awakened and revealed in periods of turmoil, e.g., the French Revolution, the Russian Revolution, and in every social upheaval which is created through the excitement of ressentiment. In other words, ressentiment is the living revolutionary force in humanity that is awakened like the sleeping lion, who in peaceful moments is easily forgotten, and all but a few of the wise have passed over his existence. If ressentiment is the repressed power for revenge in a society in which conflict is necessary and normal, then it bears in it the aggression and hatred in which destructiveness, perversity and distortion find their primordial beginnings, their capacity to be political forces against those sublimating powers of law, nobility and spiritual equanimity.

Ressentiment found its classical expression in Nietzsche's *Genealogy of Morals: A Polemic,* and there we confront the paradox of impotence and the intensity of hatred, i.e., in impotence we discover the source of "the most spiritual and poisonous kind of hatred" and vengefulness. If we can change the references in Nietzsche's descriptions, the objects of his scorn, we can bring forth a doctrine of ressentiment which is extremely valuable today and forces us to reconsider our most important ethical problems. What Nietzsche has done in his comprehension of ressentiment is to force us to rethink the problems of politics and ethics. Ressentiment is an ethical problem simply because it reveals the deepest consequences of our political and economic inequalities and turns us toward the spiritual upsurge, the volcanic force that lives within the separation and conflicts that divide the rich from the poor, the haves from the have-nots. From Nietzsche we grasp the spiritual power that grows in impotency. In recognizing that impotency can be the source from which such power can arise is already a serious and significant transformation of ressentiment into potency for social change. Its impotence breeds ideas of turmoil, hate and revenge. It declares an imaginative war against its foes and awaits its leader. Its imagination is vivid and fruitful, clearly evocative, bearing within itself a logic of expression. Here we have no oddities of thought or chaotically spoken phrases, here in the impotence of ressentiment an abundance of feelings emerges which will one day be imposed upon mankind with a clearly developed ideology. Harbored and suppressed through the years these feelings arise volcanicly when the peculiarity of time favors their manifestation or when the political leader forces them into political power.

Following Nietzsche's further description of the peculiar and distinct place of Israel in history we face the polemical question that surpasses all others in its imaginative quality and ferocious condemnation. "Did Israel not attain the ultimate goal of its sublime vengefulness precisely through the bypath of this 'Redeemer,' this ostensible opponent and disintegrator of Israel?"[3] What Nietzsche called "sublime vengefulness" transcended the power of our representational capacity. This vengefulness can only be grasped by our reason as a metaphor having no concrete corresponding actuality in experience. We work with metaphors and symbols in and through which we attempt to grasp the reality of ressentiment. Whether we are attracted by Nietzsche's interpretation of Jewish-Christian relations is beyond the point. What is significant is that ressentiment lies at the basis of the most serious and devastating social and political turmoils. Israel's "sublime vengefulness" was manifest in her struggle with paganism, with the orgiastic rites of the Baal worshippers, with every attempt to modify radical monotheism, to elevate the finite to the infinite, to deify nature, to reduce philosophy to pantheism. The struggle against paganism was a spiritual revenge that lasted for centuries drawing into itself the most precious heritage of Hellenism, its aesthetic beauty and its moral humanism. The victory of the "Redeemer" transformed Israel's impotency to the victorious potency of universal love whose origin was "sublime hatred."

Nietzsche's question evolved into a further one: "Was it not part of the social black art of a truly *grand* politics of revenge, of a farseeing, subterranean, slowly advancing, and premeditated revenge, that Israel must itself deny the real instrument of its revenge before all the world as a mortal enemy and nail it to the cross, so that 'all the world' namely all the opponents of Israel, could unhesitatingly swallow just this barb?"[4] Israel which suffers the opposition of the peoples in their paganism lives from the revenge of her unique and incomparable God. Alone among the nations she, in her impotency, can not bring her God to the world without mockery, hatred and scorn. Christianity carries forth Israel's ressentiment under the guise of love. This is the love of intolerance for the ideals of humanity, its love of scepticism, its sensibility to moderation, its proclivity and esteem for prudence and its sense of limitation. Christianity has the Judaic mission: the fierce and violent extirpation of paganism with its validation of physical beauty, of human dignity, of political and social life as the sole source of man's education to cultural maturity. "What is certain, at least," Nietzsche remarked, "is that *sub hoc signo* Israel with its vengefulness and revaluation of all values, has hitherto triumphed again and again over all other ideals, over all nobler ideals."[5]

It was important for Nietzsche to emphasize the fact that the "Redeemer" did not grow from "the denial of the thirst for revenge, as the opposite of Jewish hatred. No, the reverse is true! That love grew out of it as its crown, as its triumphant crown spreading itself farther and farther into the purest brightness...."[6] What constitutes the continuous struggle between Judaism and Christianity depends upon how deeply they recognize each other in their differences, in the indeterminable and unfathomable incapacity of each to find in the other the ressentiment that lies at the base of both faiths. Ressentiment is also a reevaluation of values; it proclaims that the "suffering, deprived, sick, ugly alone are the pious," it ennobles what is not noble, it dignifies what no longer has dignity. In the name of a divinity, of an ideology and a myth ressentiment engages those whose opposition to society bears within it society's destruction. Where and when society creates the conditions in which ressentiment grows it creates those groups which, cut off from society, no longer have obligations toward it and easily tear from it the fabric of its stability. New values are declared in the name of social and economic justice, the disguise for the man of ressentiment. Whatever gives society its cohesion becomes the creator of its foes, class, struggles against class, race against race and terror infuses its chaos when order is held sacred and defended. Ressentiment justifies its action, where action is possible, because of its suffering impotence, the blame it places on the ruling class clears the way for its directors to transfigure the impotency into adjectival forms of history and class struggle.

Love comes forth from this impotency and belongs to it in an organic way. From sublime and profound hatred, confounded at first, by the possibilities of such ties between sublimity and hatred, love, with which Christianity conquered and dominated the world emerges. This love bears within it the source of its life: Christian vengeance and hatred. This is a conquering and dominating love which crushes its rivals, transforms and transfigures reality in its image, knows the burning truth of its faith consumes all that oppose it, reduces the natural and finite world to a momentary path in the journey to salvation. Deep within its attitude is the ressentiment which it inherited from the Jews. This is the ressentiment which is against the sufficiency of natural life, against its abandonment of the super-natural, against the autonomous adequacy of morality and aesthetics, against the self-satisfaction that can accompany the finitude of human life. What is deeply significant is the realization that every form of life breeds in it the ressentiment of those for whom other forms are necessary, for whom societal conditions are not adequate and who therefore envision their misfortunes to be the work of others. There are those whose visions face a recalcitrant world and who in bitter opposition and in stubborn refusal to surrender build their ressentiment toward the world in which they dwell. It is from this ressentiment that we comprehend the history of revolution, the natural state of war, the search for power, that exists not only between individuals but between groups. These are the potential wars that lie in the impotence of those groups who for the moment have discovered no means to express their inadequacies. Knowing that its emergence is dependent upon forces which understand the depths of its potentiality and can stir its potencies and give them form ressentiment is a powerful feeling easily used by a leader. If we grasp the fact that this actual impotency bears within it a vast and immeasurable potency then the dimensions of its dangers can overwhelm our sense of proportion and play havoc with our concept of order and value. Faced with this transvaluation of values, this source of violence and negation, which we call the "slave revolt in morality," we are forced to rethink the traditions which gave us our traditional values.

Nietzsche had the "good fortune" to be able to paint his descriptions with broad sweeps of the pen. For that reason we feel as if we stand before a picture to be appreciated for its wondrous lines, colors and relationships. We are pleased or displeased, we admire or turn away, but we neither say yes nor no. We mull it over like an impression that does not go away, but also does not suffocate. With Nietzsche we breathe in his impressions and juggle their validity. Their value grows or is diminished and we must return again and again to the museum of his paintings for new impressions. With his words we are captivated and liberated at the same time. "From the profoundest and sublimest kind of hatred, Jewish hatred—ideals and reversing values, the like of which has never existed on earth before — there grew something equally incomparable, a new love, the profoundest and sublimest kind of love —

and from what other trunk could it have grown?"⁷

Here we stand in wonder at a triumph that seems never to have happened. The victory of the "Redeemer" is a fantasy. Israel's ressentiment grows deeper as paganism advances with its myths of master races, the dreams of classless society, the false prophets of millennial imagery and those who envision schemes of history which divorce us radically from political and individual responsibility. With amusement we contemplate the three simple words, *sub ho signo* and we realize that ressentiment has deeper roots than Israel, that it is infected with social dogmas which exploit and distort social and political inequalities that have torn at the foundations of societies from the earliest time of human history when democrats warred against aristocrats and when we accepted the fact that conflict created human society and that in every society the divisions and wars between groups constituted that natural law of societal life.

The slave revolt morality was intimately tied to ressentiment. Nietzsche believed that this revolt became meaningful when ressentiment in its impotency became potent and called forth values. He defined this ressentiment as that "of natures that are denied the true reaction, that of deeds, and compensate themselves with an imaginary revenge. While every noble morality develops from a triumphant affirmation of itself, slave morality from the outset says No to what is 'outside,' what is 'different,' what is 'not itself;' and this No is its creative deed."⁸

The imaginary revenge that is born in ressentiment is indeed different from what Nietzsche called the "value-positing eye," but in the depths of its imagination lay intense volcanic powers which needed articulation and found them in the communicative imagery of myth and ideology. This imagery released the aggressiveness that accompanied ressentiment in its painful but fruitful impotency. Ressentiment, Nietzsche observed, needs a "hostile external world" which is the opposite of the "noble mode of valuation." Ressentiment takes as its opponent the idealistic misconception of human nature.

If ressentiment lives from its description of the hostile external world, from its refusal to limit man's unfathomable and undetermined capacities for aggression and destruction, from its realization that man is an "open question" then it discovers more and more of his nature in conflict, in the struggle between friend and foe. Ressentiment is the state of nature in which man finds himself at the moment that he becomes conscious of himself as an active being, as a possessor of that natural malice which makes human life comprehensible. In denying the possibility that man can dominate the malice that is concomitant with ressentiment, and recognizing the legitimacy of the natural state of conflict we begin to realize that if in conflict we find the state of nature then it is ressentiment which is the natural state of consciousness from which man begins to construct his societal and national life. If Israel taught sublime vengeance, as Nietzsche thought, and left this legacy to Christianity, then what was taught was not the ideal significance of Israel or Christianity but the meaning of ressentiment as the foundation of religious life. In revenge, which we can better designate as malicious struggle, begins that critical battle between the potent and impotent thoughts which live with each other in conflict, each waiting to submerge the other, each dependent upon the powers of the imagination, the depths of sublimated suffering and the mythical and ideological framework in which the ideology of this suffering is communicated. In this framework emerges man's belief that he controls reality. He has given form to it. With this form man finds that his thought is not only a mental construct but a reality that bears within itself powers to demolish all forms. The creative powers of man's ideological passions are so strong that they assume divine force. In them man is captured by the experience that his thinking is being.

The man of ressentiment Nietzsche told us, is "neither upright nor naive nor honest and straightforward with himself. His soul squints; his spirit loves hiding places, secret paths and back doors, everything covert entices him as *his* world, *his* security, *his* refreshment; he understands how to keep silent, how not to forget, how to wait.... A race of such men of *ressentiment* is bound to become eventually *cleverer* than any noble race."[9]

Ressentiment has become the hidden feelings of the underprivileged, of those who consider themselves oppressed, of those who feel deprived and perverted, but from all this they have learned to be clever, to forget nothing and be allured by the secret call, the underground, the revolutionary; they have learned how to squint. From this ressentiment a new morality has emerged, the morality of immorality and amorality. They have been taught to forget morality, they have cleansed themselves of conscience and consciousness. Ressentiment has left behind

Jewish hatred and the sublimity of its vengeance.

The contemporary world, beyond Nietzsche's imagination, has given ressentiment a scope of development never before imagined. From its depths of cleverness it has produced the modern dictators and their imagery of class struggle, racism, charismatic leadership, holy wars and sacrificial religious heroism. Ressentiment has built the ideology of mass struggle. It has become the weapon of mass revolt. In the transvaluation of values it has deeply and perilously threatened the values of the Enlightenment, the classical values of Hellenism and the universal expression of reason alive in the Idea of Humanity. Ressentiment rises up against them not to confront but to destroy them. The sublime hatred and vengeance of old now yields to the clever vengeance and manipulated hatred of the suppressed. With this cleverness the moral world of human freedom and truth is not only threatened, but mortally wounded. Cleverness is amoral; it feels comfortable with the immoral because it refuses to separate the truth from the lie. It joins them together in such a way that every distinction between them is lost.

Ressentiment not only gives forth the clever, the covetous, the unforgetting, it grows from the decay of political conditions and racial injustice. It gives forth forceful ideas and passions. In this respect Nietzsche made some remarkable observations about Jews in *Daybreak, Morgenroete,* which he published in 1881. There he asked about the consequences of Jewish history:

> whether . . . this abundance of passions, virtues, decisions, renunciations, struggles, victories of every kind—whither shall it stream out if not at least into great men—and great works! . . . When Israel will have transformed its eternal vengeance into an eternal blessing for Europe then there will again arrive that seventh day in which the ancient Jewish God may rejoice in himself, his creation and his chosen people—and let us all rejoice with him.[10]

From the hate the Jews knew the pagan world held toward them, from the scorn which Christianity leveled against them, they developed an inner strength and power which gave them eternity, the realization that they were one with the divine manifestation. Only when Christianity understood that it belonged eternally to Israel did it know that they both fought the same enemy: the Gnostic duality which achieved its highest manifestation in Leninism. From their wars against the Baalim with the sexual immoralities that corrupted the fabric of human society to their life and death struggle against modern Gnosticism, Israel was able to give to the world the possibility of the moral Idea although she bore within herself that sublime hatred and revenge that made her survival a possibility.

One of the most devastating consequences of ressentiment is the dualism between truth and the lie which emerged in Leninism and has profoundly determined the politics of the contemporary world. In a sense it is this dualism that has transvalued the morality of Western civilization. Clearly and forcefully this volcanic upheaval in values was delineated by the Jesuit scholar Gaston Fessard and elaborated with amazing precision by Alain Besançon in his *Les Origines intellectuelles du Leninism* and *La Confusion des langues* both published in 1978. Besançon constructed Machiavelli's ontological monism with Lenin's ontological dualism to show the fundamental break in moral and political perspectives achieved by them. He states: "Machiavelli's ontological monism makes possible the opposition of the lie and the truth within the same reality. The truth describes the common reality; the lie distorts and perverts it. There is a doubling of language. The truth and the lie have their seat in the heart of the same subject who, with the freedom of will, chooses to be truthful or to lie. If he lies he is divided because he continues to shelter within himself the awareness of truth. There is, consequently, only one meaning. Lenin's ontological dualism reverses the situation. There is no longer truth in itself. There is no longer freedom. Lenin would immediately reply: Truth for whom, freedom for whom? There is no common reality. There are two truths in mortal competition each attached to its objective *camp:* bourgeois truth for the bourgeoisie, proletarian truth for the proletariat. There is, however, no symmetry and even less equality between the two truths. The truth of the proletariat is guaranteed by the future; the truth of the bourgeoisie belongs to the past and is absorbed in it and falsified. Proletarian knowledge (*science*) comprehends that of the bourgeoisie, but the latter does not comprehend the former."[11]

No longer does the metamorphosis of values remain an abstraction, a poetic metaphor which delights the imagination of the philosopher. Here it has found its incarnation and with it has confounded a world whose language is incapable of grasping such an inversion of reality. In this lies the possible weakness of an ethic that has always assumed an ontological monism. What does it mean to confront a dualism whose doubling of language becomes a perversion to those who remain firm in their belief that the lie is the distortion of truth and that truth and truthfulness are the basis of a reasonable world in search of freedom. In gnostic dualism higher truth devalues other assumed truths, plays havoc with them and destroys their validity.

To further illustrate the inversion of values brought about by Lenin's gnosticism Besançon pointed to the differences in the role of faith between our religious tradition and that of Lenin. He states:

> At the sacrifice of Isaac, Abraham "believed" what God told him. Before the empty tomb, John "believed." In the Koran the word faith means, as in the Bible, to rely upon someone, to confide in someone. Fundamental to the religions of faith there is a conscious *non known,* a *non-su.* Abraham, St. John, Mohammed knew that they did not know. They knew only that they believed. When Lenin declares that the materialistic conception of history is not a hypothesis but a scientifically demonstrated doctrine, it is certainly a belief, but he supposes it proven and based upon experience. At the basis of the ideology there is a known. Lenin does not know that he believes. He believes that he knows.[12]

What we discover here is the meaning of the transvaluation of values. Nietzsche had spoken of it poetically and we observed his remarks and descriptions from a distance. We feel that we are watching a drama of descriptive imageries rather than being forced to come to terms with reality. We feel as if we could leave Nietzsche and return to creaturely comforts after the excitement is over. With Lenin and later Stalin and Hitler we were no longer in the theatre. We faced living movements of revolutionary force whose duration and terror could no longer be avoided. We began to realize that we were experiencing more than traditional tyranny, oppression, and despotism, but conscious political and social attempts to change man's nature through perversion of language, law, history and a dualistic ontology. We were witness to the political concretization of new gnosticisms. The men of ressentiment had become creators of the new man and the new morality. Once again a fierce dualism had emerged in language and thought and we felt inadequate with our traditional language and ways of thinking to seriously face this new gnosis. Dualism is comprehensible as long as it remains ethical and temporal, i.e., experiential and contingent. It becomes destructive when it becomes metaphysical and cosmic, when it forces upon us the truth of the metaphysical reality of the two truths.

Ressentiment causes men to feel themselves returned to natural, i.e., biological conditions from which legal restrictions become artificial restraints. Nietzsche remarked justly "that from the highest biological standpoint, legal conditions can never be other than *exceptional conditions* since they constitute a partial restriction of the will of life, which is bent upon power and are subordinate to its total goal as a single means: namely, as a means of creating greater units of power."[13] Ressentiment in the depths of its impotence is a will to power, the will of life which grows in intensity with the forces of its suppression. The revenge that grows from and with hatred and malice becomes the leaven which in time will stream forth with terrifying power to destroy all that lies before it. When we conjure up the name of Hitler we have images of destruction, torture and perversity. In his *Mein Kampf* he had written: "What free time I had left from my work was spent on my studies. In a few years I thus created for myself the basis of the knowledge on which I still feed. During that time I formed a picture of the world and an ideology which has become the granite foundation of my deeds. I only had to add a little more knowledge to that which I had acquired at that time; I did not have to revise anything."[14]

The picture of the world formed by a man of ressentiment embodied in it a simple but clear division between good and evil, between the love of a fantasy that imaged a chosen heroic race and a terrifying hatred of democracy, cosmopolitanism, Marxism and Jewry. The dualism of one man is insignificant until it incarnates itself into a nation who follows him eagerly and carries through the consequences of his visions. The German historian Karl Dietrich Bracher calls it the "terrible disease of modern nationalism whose desire for exclusivity and war against everything 'alien' constitutes one of the root causes of anti-Semitism."[15]

Without the sophistication of Lenin, Hitlerism demonstrates the same love of dualism, the same conviction that beliefs were scientifically demonstrable truths and that cleverness and hatred had become the supreme virtue. Hatred and scorn had become metaphysical and physical forces which bore within themselves political and social consequences whose meaning comes forth in the struggle for power through a radical upheaval of societal life. The idolatry and orgiastic sexuality which obliterated the sense of justice and truthfulness and which in biblical history formed the character of Israel's unique struggle against Paganism now turned toward Israel with a vehemence which can be explained through thousands of years of ressentiment. Israel was now identified with the truth of Christianity. Israel's destruction was inseparable from that of Christianity. The Paganism that was characteristic of both Nazism and Communism produced a monstrous form of ontological dualism: master race, class struggle, racial and class hatred. From ressentiment it drew its incredible strength.

Nietzsche, who knew ressentiment well, spoke of it in the second part of *Thus Spake Zarathustra*. In it he wrote a parable about the Tarantulas. He began his parabolic tale with this description: "There it comes willingly: welcome, tarantula! Your triangle and symbol sits black on your back and I also know what sits in your soul. Revenge sits in your soul: wherever you bite, black scabs grow; your poison makes the soul whirl with revenge."[16]

Nietzsche once remarked that philosophers think either with their heads or their souls and that he belonged to those of the soul. The representational form of his thinking makes us uneasy about the seriousness of his philosophy, but for those of us who still have not sought truth exclusively in the sign Nietzsche's imagery is serious business. Revenge lives in the soul in man's being as naturally as the biological functioning of bodily operations. There are always oppositions, conflicts and distasteful worlds and peoples about us. We emerge into reality within groups of friends and foes, with war as the natural condition of life, with the oppressed and the oppressors creating the nourishment for ideologies and myths to enunciate their existence, their right to power and conquest.

Where revenge is evoked, the slave morality is armed for struggle, there the leader, the party, the force of history has moved to the center stage and impotency yields the intensity of its emotive power. *"That man be delivered from revenge,* that is for me the bridge to the highest hope and a rainbow after long storms."[17] Nietzsche spoke of deliverance from revenge because he knew that in revenge man loses what is most noble in him: the sense of his dignity. From revenge rode forth those crushing millennial schemes of redemption that were in essence human destruction. Revenge cut itself free from that ontological monism which preserved man's hopes to build in life those heights from which he could declare his nobility and beauty. With revenge man transforms justice. He reduces all values to those of the man of ressentiment. "We shall wreak vengeance and abuse on all whose equal we are not,"[18] speaks the man of ressentiment. Since we are not capable of doing it physically the vengeance which we will bring forth grows with intensity as we ponder our impotency. This impotence we share with all men, in all time. Ressentiment is the primal condition of human finitude. Nothing makes us more forcefully aware of our inadequacies and insufficiencies than the realization that we are incapable of realizing from ourselves the overcoming of the barriers which make us unequal to our fellow man. We are unequal in the natural inequality of human capacities, opportunities and achievements, we are unequal in the structures and organizations of human societies that privilege some to the detriment of others. In our inequality we discover the meaning of ressentiment, the forces of conflict which emerge from it and condition the nature of human society. Behind the Hobbesian world of natural war, silent and vocal, ressentiment conditions the quality of man's existence in a world whose law is inequality and the will to power.

From this world ideologies grow with intensity in finesse and novelty. Man's power of invention is fed with the impotency of ressentiment. Their relation is necessary and mutually productive. We remain unaware of the inventive consequences of impotence. There is a fear and anxiety before these unknown forces and we possess a reactive power which we must believe will be inadequate to the undefinable forces of ressentiment. The renewed power of the lie, its ontological independence, has disoriented our political thinking. Besançon remarked that "the disorientation of reason, the privation of references, the self-assurance of the ideological assertion, the absolute division between what is said and what is, is revealed with the incomparable aid of secret power. Since it is ideology which permits this expression of power and draws near the moment when it will be realized, it is what is true. The total power of the lie proves once again the vivacity of ideology. Through it we enter the realm of the False."[19]

From the ideology of the double truth that is infused in the monistic ontology of bourgeois thought the Leninist dialectic is able to comprehend the different truths of the bourgeoisie and the proletariat as moments of a process in which affirmation and negation become interchangeable. To what we say yes, we can also negate, and what we negate we can also affirm. This sophistic dualism emerges as the revenge of slaves upon the masters. The truth and the lie of the masters depend upon the truth of the proletariat class. What is effective as truth is the lie, what is effective as the lie is the truth. We expect the lie but are unprepared for the truth. Besançon reminded us that the paradox is explained by the fundamental dissymmetry provoked by the introduction into a monistic world of dualist thinking. Bourgeois politics sees a duplicity, a duplication of thinking where, from a Leninist perspective. there is a duplication of reality. For reason Leninism does engage "in a ruse when it refuses to proceed by *sic et non,* yes yes or no no. It posits the yes and the no as two moments of a process whose law it knows and which is called dialectic. Its good faith is totally in the one as it is in the other. Illuminated by the doctrine, led by the mode of thinking it does not comprehend the incomprehension of its ally. It accuses him of bad faith."[20] This political dualism which now refuses distinctions between the lie and the truth manifests the same disregard for the monism of western civilization. Dualism knows no ethical distinction between what *is* and what *ought to be,* between the meaning of the future in relation to the difference from the past and the present.

We face what Nietzsche called the frenzy of revenge. He wrote: "Aggrieved concert, repressed envy... perhaps the concert and envy of your fathers... erupt from you as a flame and as the frenzy of revenge. What was silent in the father speaks in the son; and often I found in the son the unveiled secret of the father."[21]

With whatever terms we describe the character of the man of ressentiment we cannot avoid what Nietzsche called repressed envy, frenzied revenge, sublime or distorting hatred, cleverness and whatever other form of destructiveness which is liberated in those who need to bring havoc and terror into the body politic. They bear within themselves the "tyrannomania" of impotence which seeks to free itself of its impotence. There is no reconciliation with the enthusiast, with the warrior of faith, with those who refuse to think, with those for whom there are no values, not even those of a dualist world view. Wherever there is a power-impulse to power, to injustice, to punishment there we must act with caution, there we are reduced to the acts of revenge, but in our reduction we remain morally conscious of what we do.

How do we face the powers which live within ressentiment, whose delineation we are incapable of making and whose dangers are beyond our measures? Philosophy must speak from the concreteness of the human situation, its politics, its morality and its struggle for knowledge. In this concreteness it seeks to find reasonable guides for human action in an indifferent world, for human relationships where conceit, envy, distortion never fail to exercise influence and strength. We find it difficult to avoid the natural malices that afflict man's nature. We must always come to terms with sinful men. Our struggle for virtue, for friendship would be meaningless if "radical evil" did not force man to find ways to overcome his inclination to perversity, to a mistrust of his fellowman and to his realization that his dominance over his passions is inadequate. Most threatening is the radical dualism which has emerged in Soviet Communism: the interplay between the truth and the lie, the subordination of morality to political power. With the growth of ideology, the most characteristic quality of our contemporary civilization, we have witnessed an upheaval in our language. The transvaluation of values is brought about through language, through the ability of the ideologue to change meaning, to reinterpret word significance in such a way that traditional distinctions fade and differences cease. With the ability to accept the first societal lie the process moves quickly. Truth and lie fade into each other. This is possible when power is the supreme reality. Where philosophers speak we should hear the voice of reason, the unifying force of the concept, the vision of the Idea; where power speaks reality is no longer questioned and discussed, but the weight and strength of ideology commands. There is intellectual strength in Ideas, but power in the state. Lenin knew this well and he remarked that all "the reality of ideology is concentrated in the exercise of power. Only on this level do rational, instrumental and ideologically neutral behaviors exist. They are enveloped and provided by ideology with an efficacy that these behaviors did not have in the chilly Machiavellianism of the past. At this level we find the traditionally human passions for governing, dominating and more generally, for action which are transcended by ideology but are also, because of it, amply satisfied. Leninist power, like all power, is drawn from the real, attacked and eaten from it and can hope to be nourished by it. The passion for power which authorizes ideology is a means of escaping from the unreality of ideology."[22] From this identification of power and ideology the traditional values and attitudes of Western society meet their deepest challenge. Their values have always sought to control power, to find values that supersede and limit it.

The philosopher is compelled to know what is happening in the world about him. It is unimaginable for him to be oblivious to the implications of the Nazi state or that of Soviet communism, to believe that his theoretical problem are devoid of political and moral consequences. The philosopher belongs to his time, i.e., to its politics, morality, science. When we think of the meaning of ressentiment, revenge, of dualistic ontology, religious fanaticism, nationalism, we turn to ourselves and ask: what is to be done? what are the alternatives in ideological thinking? what are the political and moral commitments that must be made in the struggle for freedom? We know these commitments have had deepest influence upon the actions of the self. The fundamental commitment to truth and freedom remains firm and serious and even though we feel that this is vague, and perhaps inadequate, we know that it can be so profoundly rooted in us that its external abstractness in no way corresponds to its internal concreteness. Ideology has grown to tremendous proportions and its effectiveness has also developed through clarification and delineation. There are problems in the most refined ideological expressions. In their manifestations the possibilities and probabilities which they affect in man's existence raises as many unexpected problems as it would in less ideologically controlled societies. Man's natural malice remains, even if differently organized and directed. Man's struggle for power, his natural covetousness and envy give forth ever new forms that are dangerous even for the most highly organized ideological society. Even nature plays her forceful role when she manipulates our finiteness and makes the most haughty humble, the most certain of men aware of the folly of such confidence. There is also the weight of our traditional philosophy and our belief in its efficacy. Whatever men bring forth to startle us with their possibility and malice, their destructiveness and cleverness, we find in our belief in freedom a fact which is firm and resistant. We discern in this faith the humanity of our fellowman, the Idea of the human community and man's capacity for compassion.

In an article which Fritz Kaufmann contributed to the volume on Karl Jaspers for the *Library of Living Philosophers* he remarked about the absence of compassion in Jaspers and its central role in Hermann Cohen. He stated:

> In the Bible this latter love (the correlation between man and man which has its actuality in the correlation between man and God) is kindled by compassion which is so little in evidence in Jaspers' writings. There is, however, compassion in all human love, since there is suffering in all human beings. It is through compassion according to Cohen, that the "other" being becomes my "fellow" being with whom I bear and for whom I live.[23]

Does this not sound vague and inadequate before the ideological realism of Lenin, the Ressentiment of Scheler and Nietzsche who fought so diligently against compassion? The yes and the no can be given only when we explore in some detail Cohen's remarks. They will never be acceptable to the sceptic or those already convinced of the efficacy of ideology and for whom the ideologue has given a final answer.

Philosophy, for Cohen, was more than theoretical speculation; it was an exploration of man's moral responsibility to his fellowman and in this sense to the Idea of Humanity. In fact, it was his discovery of fellowman that Cohen, in his last work, *Religion of Reason* brought individuality and universality together. The concept of the fellowman, he said,

> conceals a correlation of its own, namely, that of man and man, but in the narrower correlation there is merely an initial unfolding of the meaning and content of the more universal one. For the correlation of man and God cannot be actualized if the correlation of man and man is not first included . . . and since the share of religion in reason consists in its share of morality, if ethics is impossible, religion becomes also untenable; for then the correlation disintegrates; man then is no longer fellowman, the link in correlation to God, and no other concept of man but the moral concept of the fellowman can be established in this correlation.[24]

Cohen's affirmation of man's moral quality is inseparable from that of his commitment to man's relationship to God which is also moral. The quality of human life is determined by how fully the individual is able to free himself from the bonds of his sensuous individuality and reach out to the universal demands of moral life, to bring into the circle of one's existence the existence of our fellowman as one for whom I have responsibility, who needs my compassion and from whom I need a similar compassion. Cohen reminded us that "even if I had no heart in my body, my education alone would have brought me to the insight that the great majority of men cannot be isolated from me, and that I myself am nothing, if I do not make myself a part of them. In these unavoidable connections between myself and the majority, a relationship arises that means more than merely coordination or even subordination, but which produces a community. And the community produces the fellowman. The community is reciprocal action."[25]

Man's factuality is merely a starting point from which he begins his path toward humanity. In his primitive factuality he is barbaric. From this barbarism he is guided by the Idea of Humanity by a reason that is not identified with the immediacy of his feelings and needs, but which commands that he leave them. In parting from this immediacy of existence man learns to reconstruct existence from a moral universalism, he seeks to comprehend the Idea, to be guided by it as if it were the light of his eyes, *The Good*. Man begins his journey to the humanity in him by recognizing the self in the other and in being recognized as a self by the other. Here begins the story of law, the reciprocity of relationships and responsibilities we call society. Man leaves the savagery of his unrecognized and non-responsible self when in community he realizes that in moral non-recognition man reduces his fellowman to barbarism.

Together with the discovery of the fellowman is the need for compassion which transforms this discovery from the realm of logic to that of ethics. This transformation is fundamental for without it our fellowman is a mere conceptual creation, but not truly our factual fellowman whose sufferings and joys are vital to us. Here in the discovery of compassion, *Mitleid,* Cohen found the meaning of an existential philosophy. Not in logic, but in ethics we find the essence of our fellowman, not in an abstract recognition but in the facticity of his pain, his love and his search for meaning. The idealism of those who discover the fellowman in conceptualization alone is refused by Cohen who knew the power of compassion.

> Pity (compassion) should only reveal to me that the other is rather myself. Knowledge, of course, would never have brought me to this truth if it had not dawned on me in the thing-in-itself of the will, if compassion, the organ of the will had not put truth into focus. This compassion is more than knowledge, which represents merely the phenomenon. Compassion is the messenger of the will, therefore of the thing-in-itself. And this thing-in-itself means the identity of all that appears as man.[26]

Cohen believed that compassion was the revealing power of the moral world in and through which man discovers his individuality in his fellowman in the fullness and wholeness of his being. In the poverty of others man finds his social responsibility. Faced with this suffering man's compassion must be more than feeling; it must come forth as action, as community action as the social obligation of man as a societal being. Comprehending the perversion of the morally inactive individual, man realizes that society is the realm in which he realizes his potential for moral action and thought. In society he discovers his need to make decisions and participate in communal organizations.

Where compassion is absent, where social awareness does not focus on economic inequality and where political action is disregarded or debased, we discover the birth of ressentiment and that of revenge which grows in the impotency and in its search for leadership. Ressentiment becomes a reality when man is deprived of his obligation to his fellowman. Compassion makes us see that where poverty is allowed to fester and where political struggle has no moral purpose we cultivate that feeling of ressentiment which lets loose upon society forces dedicated to its destruction, because they are cut off from coherent language and are indifferent to the values it embodies. Cohen called compassion the "motor of the pure will" which transforms man from the indifferent other into the fellowman. If compassion is the "motor of the pure will," if it creates man into the fellowman then we know that only through the struggle for social and political justice, through loyalty to freedom and the search for the truth do we lessen the gaps between the privileged and the unprivileged, the franchised and the unfranchised groups among us. In compassion we moderate the ressentiment, the feeling of revenge and the catastrophic ontological dualism which negates traditional values by destroying the primordial difference between the truth and the lie. In Cohen's sense of compassion we ponder again the force of the moral will and its capacity to reconstruct reality from the fact that virtue is potential in all men and that the future is hope that the ethical will has just begun its historical adventure. The forces that oppose it weigh heavily against it, but in man's will to redeem his humanity there is an unbreakable denial of the metaphysical independence of evil. Cohen's belief in the future was the strength to fight in the present for the Idea of Humanity.

We have spoken of the political and moral dimensions of ressentiment. We have comprehended it as the volcanic source of revolution. From it has emerged the force to maintain the new ideological Gnosticism: class struggle. Formed and activated by hate, ressentiment in the depth of its impotency is the most serious threat to freedom and the search for truth. Cohen's realization that compassion toward the misfortunate is the discovery of individuality and the fellowman as the misfortune of poverty, gave the problem a wider social and economic scope by relating it to the realities discoverable in every human society. In poverty we know how painfully man can be separated from man and how in this separation he nourishes the hatreds which accompany ressentiment. Compassion is the call for healing. It calls us not to class antagonism, but to communal responsibility, not to racial hatreds, but to the valuation of the humanity in our fellowman. It calls us to both universality and individuality, to both the universal and the individual experience and it refuses to reduce us to that ideology which logically fuses both experiences into a dependence upon a preordained conflict, future, and truth. In Cohen's ethical will we discover the unique source of our peculiar individuality which remains persistently opposed to any and every system that fails to recognize its inviolability.

6

The Abyss of Contradiction: Peace and Hatred

In the last work of Hermann Cohen, *Religion of Reason out of the Sources of Judaism,* there is a short but significant chapter on "Peace." Cohen, who died in 1918, embodied in his systematic philosophy the highest achievement of Platonic and Kantian philosophy. Neither a commentator nor a historian of his predecessors, Cohen developed his own unique philosophical system in which reason reached a sublime level of speculation and systematic organization. Cohen's belief in reason accompanied his love of Monotheism and Messianism. His Judaism and philosophy were not allowed to dwell in the lands of the two truths. Cohen brought them together in such a way that the autonomy of philosophy was never threatened by the truth of ancestral faith. Each is alive where the other lives with energy and belief. If ever the *faith of reason* catapulted philosophy forward with optimism and power it was here in the spirit of Cohen, in a mind excited by the infinitesimal nature of reason and by the vast possibilities that he knew to be reality.

I have chosen to discuss the problem of hatred and peace. It meant much to Cohen and it gives us a comprehension of the problem of peace. This problem belongs to the reasonable dialogue of human beings who still are committed to the faith of reason and the universality of its reality. Hatred and peace as realities are intimately related. In speaking of one we are involved in its effect upon the other. It is in the other that we find again the wholeness which is a relationship between them but not necessary dialectic. Cohen remarked that "only through peace as the unifying force of human consciousness, is love, in all its directions, liberated from the ambiguities which are connected with it. Man ought to love his fellowman. Is he actually able to do this, this selfish man? Is human love able to exceed the few solemn moments of compassion? ... And this frail man, should he be able to love God as the archetype of his morality and of his self-perfection? Is he supposed not merely to honor and follow his ideal but also to be able to love it? Is this not simply a contradiction? And finally, God is supposed to love the children of men, in spite of their weaknesses and their sins or rather because of them, since he becomes the redeemer of their guilt of sin. How are all these meanings of love possible in themselves and reconcilable one with another?"[1] We ask the questions and we think of the answers, we reflect upon the immediacy of experience and we want to know how deeply we should allow experience to guide our attitudes. We need to believe beyond experience. As reasonable beings we know the significance of the Idea and the Ideal, the force they exercise upon life and the communities in which we dwell. Peace is man's highest goal. From Cohen's view the end of peace "designates man's virtuous path to God, the path of man's drawing near to God."[2] Peace is contentment, the belief in God's providence. Contentment contains within it a surety, the acknowledgement that there is order and that the world is reasonable. Human action has purpose whether we want to comprehend it or not. Even violence is comprehended as the threat to reason, in and through which reason becomes aware of itself as the unique opponent of violence and chaos. Contentment is the trust in reason, that uncanny confidence that we must have to prevent ourselves from being absorbed in violence, that refusal to think or to believe that man is possible without comprehension and discourse. If man refuses to think the consequence of not thinking, has he not placed thinking at the service of violence? Is there a doing from which even the consequences fade away, a doing for the sake of doing or a silence that refuses to acknowledge the world? Violence can exist for the sake of violence; thinking can succomb to purposeless action.

The question is whether we can relate hate to violence. If as we suggest violence is the cessation of communication, hatred separates person from person, it is the destruction of community. Man is returned to bestiality; he lives again in a world of myth, ideology and atavism. Cohen observed that the Bible contains a prohibition of enmity, of hatred for our fellow man. "In the first instance this prohibition is expressed in the prohibition of vengeance and resentment. Further, it is expressed in the prohibition of forbearing assistance to the enemy with regard to the preservation of his property (Exod. 23:5). Finally, it results from the fundamental regulation in the prohibition: 'Thou shalt not hate thy brother in thy heart.' (Lev. 19:17)."[3] However we want to translate these words we are certain that hatred harms not only the other, but ourselves. Belonging as we do to our fellow-men in the discourse of reason, it is in the other that we find again the wholeness which is lost in our individuality. This wholeness is the health of body and mind. We might also ask if there is companionship in violence, but when the question is asked, relationship is already a factor and a significant one. Where the end is not the respect for humanity of every man, there the human fellowship does not exist. Where man is a means, and not an end, the wholeness that is our physical and spiritual health has little meaning.

Where is the source of hatred? Is there a legitimate object for hatred? Would not idolatry and its mythology be a legitimate object of hatred? We need to destroy the modern idolatry of modern totalitarianism and we face with horror and disgust those governments that undermine human rights and perpetuate cultic practices and attitudes. We know that where there are idolators and their idols, their forms of beliefs are antagonistic to our faith in reason. If justice and courage demand that we face the reality of idolatry, "peace," Cohen said, "has nothing in common with them, and, in spite of its relative value as a virtue, peace has the task and authority to check these absolute virtues. But how can and how will peace be capable of this?"[4] How does contentment of the soul forge its way against hatred? If hatred isolates the human from itself, what ground can the contentment of the soul find to limit the violence of hatred?

"The Talmud," Cohen stated, "has discovered the concept of wanton hatred. . . . Not only should hatred not have a false cause, but it has no cause at all. Any cause for hatred is empty and vain. Hatred is always a 'wanton hatred.'"[5] Cohen followed these remarks with a startling statement: "I can remove hatred from the human heart only insofar as I do not know any enemy at all; the information and the knowledge that a man is my enemy, that he hates me, must be as incomprehensible to me as that I could hate a man, and therefore it must drop out of my consciousness."[6] We should recall that this was written in 1918 at the end of World War I. The nationalism and atavism that permeated philosophers both in France and Germany makes it hard to believe that Cohen could project this imperative: hatred must be removed from the human heart. Was Cohen, one may ask, so naive that he could believe that hatred has no cause, and if we ascribe to it a cause, it could only be "empty and vain." Cohen was a democratic socialist. He believed that Kant's philosophy provided the fundament of socialism because it declared man to be an end and not a means. These remarks, however, go beyond socialism, Kant, and the saying: I should love my enemy. How is it possible for me not to know my enemy when experience clearly shows me the enemy, and my passions seek to revenge and destroy those who have alienated and harmed me and the values that I esteem. I am told by Cohen that it is incomprehensible that I am hated and that I can hate. Actually, I know that it is comprehensible that I am hated and that I can hate. Is it our own persuasion that forces us to believe that we are hated and can hate, or are we the carnal beings who need to hate to satisfy our passions?

Cohen was convinced that hatred is an illusion. "All hatred is in vain. I deny hatred to the human heart. Therefore I deny that I have an enemy, that a man could hate me. I deny this with the same clarity of my consciousness with which I deny that I have an enemy, that I could hate a man. What is hatred? I deny its possibility. The world which intends to describe such a concept, is altogether empty."[7] These words are so compelling that they force us to react in disbelief, or to be captivated by them. It is comprehensible to state that hatred is in vain and to deny that hatred is in the human heart, but what does it mean if I know that I can hate? How can I deny that I can hate, that I have an enemy or that I can be hated? If such a denial is possible it can only mean that as a rational being hatred is impossible, as a being who has returned to bestiality hatred is a natural reaction. The moral struggle of mankind is against hatred. The categorical imperative of this struggle is my refusal to concede that I can hate a fellow being knowing at the same time that justice and courage might demand his punishment and death. What is human in a person, his reason, can be so distorted that his humanity no longer exists. Whatever the events of the world tell us they do not eliminate the truth of reason; in answering the question what is hatred, Cohen replied that he denied its possibility. He spoke as a rational individual. He did not mean to say that hatred does not exist. Cohen lived in an academic world in which anti-Semitism was not a passing moment, but a real attitude and activity.

If we would accept the possibility of hatred as a natural human condition we would then deny the possibility that the moral law speaks unequivocally and recognizes only the autonomy of its law. Hatred is a condition of the human experience but this experience is not constitutive of man's nature; it is an accidental but real condition. If we introduce hatred into man's nature then we have returned to that original evil that infected mankind and necessitated God's forgiveness, or to a philosophy of history in which good and evil remain in conflict and from which pessimism is the natural result. Even more consequential is the control and domination of society by any sort of arbitrary government justifying itself on the basis of man's evil nature. Authority is justified because man's evil must be dominated. Cohen was deeply aware of the meaning of pessimism as a destructive societal factor. Where pessimism is the political mood, there the idea of humanity has little meaning, then peace has no significance in the human soul. Pessimism is the refusal of man as a reasonable being.

We must believe that hatred can be overcome both within ourselves and in the relationship between states. The "friend-enemy relationship" is exemplified in experience; it is not justified in morality. Kant remarked in his *Metaphysics of Morals* that although men "fall into brutish vice" this "does not justify our attributing to them a disposition *characteristic of their species* any more than the stunting of some trees in the forest is a reason for making them a special *kind* of plant."[8] Even more important is Kant's reflection on the consequences of hatred: isolation from society, substituting the *sensus privatus* for the *sensus communis*. The isolation implied in the *sensus privatus* allows for the destruction of the *sensus communis*. The right to violate and harm the *sensus communis* is created and developed in the *sensus privatus*. Where the *sensus privatus* dominates there the human community is threatened and disturbed. Kant stated: "For it [suppression of books] deprives us of the greatest and most useful, though not the only means for rectifying our own thoughts by asserting them in public to see whether they agree with the understanding of other men. . . . A man who pays no attention to this criterion but obstinately recognizes private sense as already valid apart from or even in opposition to common sense is abandoned to a play of thought in which he sees, conducts and judges himself, not in a world in common, with others, but in his own world (as in dreaming)."[9] Hatred and isolation, the mad world of exaggerated self-reflection caused Cohen to link hatred and illusion and to stress their banality. Hatred belongs to our refusal to think. Hatred threatens the discourse of reason. It negates its reality. The discourse of reason must transform within itself the negative value of hatred. Reason denies hatred to preserve itself as reason, the overcoming of hatred is the ever increasing realization of reason.

The relationship between hatred and reason must not be reduced to a logical interchange of abstractions. The problem is a moral one. Our concern is the elimination of hatred, the ability of peace to command the soul. Cohen stated that "with this overcoming of hatred, with the exclusion of it from the inventory of the powers of the soul, the way opens for the peace of the soul."[10] Hatred only makes me aware of my moral limitation, of the inadequacy of my actions and feeling, the weakness of my intellectual and moral commitment to the wholeness that is peace. With hatred there is that incompleteness, that unfinished quality that permeates our actions and attitudes. Peace seems at a distance as long as hatred dominates in the world. We might dream of the possibility of securing peace for ourselves, the peace of our individual lives, but we know that there is no peace for the individual if there is none for society and the world. Peace remains a dream and a hope, but it informs us with great force, it makes us aware of how deeply hatred disturbs our being and infects it with the arbitrariness of passionate feelings. "For my own peace," Cohen said, "I need the confidence that hatred among people will be destroyed from the consciousness of mankind. Peoples do not hate one another but greed awakens envy and greed and envy delude man with an illusory image which one passes off as a power of the soul, and which one presumes to confirm as such."[11] If we are willing to admit the illusions that hate fosters, if we are capable of acknowledging the myth that hate engenders and to recognize the power and potential that these myths command, then we are distinctly able to realize that illusion is force, that its effects are profound and that the march of human beings toward self-destruction is created in illusions.

Here we see the educational problems that face mankind. The movement toward peace depends upon our struggle against hatred. From the child to the adult the dangers of myths and illusions are always present. The advance of reason is the demise of the illusion. Man is an illusion-creating being. One thing, according to Cohen, remains constant: "All hatred is vain and wanton. All hatred is nothing but illusion, nothing but the interpretation and embellishment of human baseness, which is constituted by greed and selfishness and their effect, envy."[12] Cohen knew that the battle with hatred had only just begun, he knew that it was a battle against the giants of man's imagination, his search to master his world with divine force, to forge that illusion that would give him the right to develop between the saved and the damned, to control life and death, justify the cleavage between masters and slaves. The moral belief in the law and its universality could be strengthened only if hatred remained the foe. Peace is possible only if and when this hatred died. Cohen said that we need to recognize "the illusion of a false national psychology, which in all peoples is constituted by hatred; if one recognizes in a more fundamental psychology, which is enlightened by ethics, that hatred is an illusory factor of the soul, then the greater part of the burden of sin falls from the human heart."[13] The problem of hatred creates an awareness that is justified as a critique of the human situation. It is elaborated into a critique of history. We are forced to face the power of myth-making that hatred engenders. A comprehension of man, the myth-maker, is our most vital moral obligation.

History is the source to which we turn when we want to prove something about the nature of man. Is he a carnal being driven by passion? Is he not from birth evil? Can we not look to such cliches as *eros* and *thanatos* to lead us into the secrets of the human comedy or if preferred, the human tragedy? We have heard much of Hobbes and Rousseau and their theories of man and society, but are they any more than guiding possibilities with which we attempt to organize our moral and political discourses? Cohen was more radical about history. He stated: "We no longer believe in the experience of history which passes itself off as the wisdom of history, according to which everything has been and always will be the same; individuals and peoples hate each other, and hatred is an instinctual power of human consciousness. We do not trust pessimism; we despise its wisdom, because we have understood the meaning of the world more profoundly and correctly."[14] Cohen always believed that history was the struggle for the Idea of Humanity, the overcoming of wanton hatred, the way to the highest virtue, *sophrosyne,* the peace of the soul. The pessimism which we breathe in human experience should not control our faith in reason. We live in defiance of pessimism; we raise the *should be* over against the *is*. Philosophy is the education of mankind to optimism, to belief in the Idea and the Ideal. Against what *is* and *has been* there is the future, the *will* and *shall be* of practical reason. "Pessimism is rooted in the psychological error that hatred is an ordering power in the economy of nature, as is the struggle for existence which destroys countless germs in order to eliminate them from the contest. Although we do not deny the tendency to destruction, as little as we deny the elimination of the inferior germs, we distinguish the animate from everything material, even in the organic, and we reject the analogy between the two spheres, between that of nature and that of the moral world, as a will-o'-the wisp."[15] The analogies to which we have been subjected fail to comprehend that leap that is required to reach the human. Man's moral reality is his distinction, that he is affected by the Idea, that he universalizes his knowledge, that he can inhabit the moral world of responsibility and autonomy, necessitates the recognition that the will and feeling are the sources of man's highest achievements, the ethical and aesthetic consciousness. When we think of the education of mankind, we come to terms with the unity of consciousness. From within this unity we speak of the discourse of mankind, the autobiography of man's reason, where history is our valued heritage.

We cannot allow the belief that it is hatred that conditions human actions. Many would object and say that we only have to observe human beings to discover that they are driven by vanity, envy and greed. Our moralists tell us innumerable tales of vice, passion and jealousy. History announces its wars of aggression, statesmen are the manipulators of power and pride. The consequence, if assumed to be the fate of man, would be resignation and hopelessness. Throughout the human tale there has been moral opposition, the cry for social justice, the end of war, the painful hope for peace. Cohen would say: "Just as man is able to conceive of virtue, just as he is able to conceive of peace, so is he able to unmask the deadly image of hatred."[16] Man can root out what is destructive. He is not a child of fate, a marionette whose actions are determined by sordid uncontrollable power. He is not the subject of the *Eumenides*. Man is free and responsive morally. This freedom is the substance, the reality of philosophy. In Cohen's world, like in ours, the task of philosophy remains the autonomous quality of freedom.

Peace is a power. As an ideal it commands those for whom its reality has become consciousness. In the *Sayings of the Fathers* we are told to be "the disciple of Aaron loving peace and pursuing peace." We can despairingly fold our arms and leave philosophy, we can proclaim its uselessness. This is a viable option, and many take it. As long as there is a belief in reason there will be those who will demand the right to believe, the "right to dream" to hold in honor man's imagination as the essence of knowledge. Before peace, hatred dies, it has no place to root itself, no part of the soul in which it is to develop and feed. In our civilization the philosophers were supposed to be the guardians of our values. They often fail. At times they raised their hands in Nazi salutes, some sold their souls for academic privileges, turned on their teachers when they discovered that they were no longer in favor or practiced the wrong religions; they accepted ideologies that erased the Idea of Mankind to satisfy ambitions and academic advancement. Some grasped illusion and myths of race and state that contradicted their commitment to the *sensus communis* and the moral law. Many listened to and spoke the hatred of their political leaders, they reduced their religious beliefs to state policy and beliefs. The philosophers destroyed a civilization with their attachments and enchantments with totalitarianism. Cohen, with his few followers, were grains of defiance of the tide that sank into pessimism and historical destiny.

When the philosopher assumes and follows his cultural responsibility he becomes the disciple of Aaron. He is convinced that "the ghost of hatred will disappear into nothingness before his sight. Peace is that power of the soul which scares away and annihilates all the ghosts that threaten morality and the purity of the soul. Pessimism is such a ghost of rationalism and idealism."[17] Cohen's concern with pessimism did not arise in his last work. It is not as if it were the brooding of an old philosopher who had witnessed the rabid nationalism of four years of conflict, who was now pondering his battle against anti-Semitism and who viewed with despair the dying cries of the Enlightenment, and who foresaw the end of Idealism, of Neo-Kantianism in his colleague Paul Natorp, and its final demise in Martin Heidegger. Cohen always believed that pessimism was the end of philosophy as an educational force. Holding dearly to the future for his belief in the betterment of mankind, and in the untold and hardly imagined advances in knowledge and moral purity, Cohen, like all those who value his perspective, knew that the antagonist was cultural pessimism, the return to myth, fate, and historical determinism, the denial of Messianism and its universality.

Pessimism is an "inspiration of mysticism." With this thought Cohen touched the vital chord of the power of pessimism. Pessimism is the retreat from the world, from the work of the Creator, God. The creation is the work of an evil force from which we must escape to a new God. This God we approach when we free ourselves of the contamination of this evil creation and its God. The body is discarded and the spirit is liberated. The flesh is mortified and the soul purified. The contamination in which we live demands redemption and new gods, new myths, new illusions. Hatred of creation and its God begins the redeeming process. The conquerors are the mystic heroes, the saviors who give us new eschatologies and ideologies. Pessimism is the new gnosticism, it is the source of the theogonies that in their organic processes join good and evil. In the organic process the divine and the human are linked in intimacy to crush the ethical and the moral demand of the future. The qualitative distinction of time fades, the past is the future, and the future is already the past and the present. The cycle replaces the logic of the infinitesimal.

Opposed to this revived gnosticism is the power of Messianism, that hope for redemption that feeds every soul that is convinced that the moral struggle is the fundamental human concern. Redemption is that request for strength to remain firm in our optimism. Cohen remarked that "if world peace is the innermost belief of the religious consciousness, then peace must be an unfailing power, a reliable guide of the mind. In the testimony of religion, peace is the characteristic of the historical world."[18] If we affirm that peace is "characteristic of the historical world" do we not blind ourselves to the nature of the political, the friend-enemy conflict or to the natural state of conflict that exists among states in the absence of an imposing authority? The problem is whether peace is the natural situation, and conflict and hatred its negation. Peace is the end which man must discover if he is to find who he *is*. Man in search of peace is in search of himself. How sublime man is when he approaches himself, when he struggles to find that peace that creates the community of reason, that discourse of reason and the reasonable in which the human potentiality awakens to its form, to the beauty of its architecture, to the magnificence of its possibility. The problem of peace is the contradiction of the gnostic search for the separation of corporeality and spirituality. Peace is wholeness, that health, *salubriter* in which creation finds form in the law, in both corporeal beauty, and reason's principles and ideas. The creation is the source in which man finds beauty and sublimity in both body and soul.

We can now look again at hatred. Cohen was clear in intention when he wrote that "all disturbance and doubt of peace are impediments to the life of the soul; they are misinterpretations and pathological aberrations. The fundamental power of the human soul is as certainly peace as peace is the goal of human history."[19] If peace were an abstraction we could not be moved by it, but peace moves the human soul, accompanied by the feeling of joy, that emotion which we feel when we observe good actions, when we know that the humanity in us is enhanced. There is a joy in the advancement of humanity in us. We know how important it is to cultivate moral feeling, to learn to appreciate goodness and generosity. Education has little meaning if it were to neglect the feelings; it is efficacious when it attempts to cultivate sympathy for beauty, respect for virtue and awe before the moral law. Cohen rightly compared the meaning of joy and suffering when he said that the one like the other created a community of feeling. Joy is as indispensable to moral life as compassion and suffering. How deeply pleasing it is to share joy in man's achievements, to take pride in the human capacity to overcome obstacles, to defy fate and myth with messianic hope and trust. Each of us who has striven for peace knows that we must not only face its enemies but encourage and advance every opportunity to widen reasonable discourse. "Peace in man is the longing for the good in man."[20] We could put these words into the essence of philosophy and say that the purpose of philosophy is peace, the profound joy that accompanies every philosophical attempt to comprehend the known and unknown possibilities of reason, to experience the venture into the feelings and will that allow man to be moved by beauty and sublimity and to be committed to the moral law as the truth of his rational nature.

If we wanted to bring together our thoughts on peace we would say with Cohen that "peace is the unity of all vital powers, their equilibrium and reconciliation of all their contradictions. Peace is the crown of life."[21] When we say this about peace there is nobility in it that at first seems to immobilize us. We are in awe before the sublimity of the words; the task is too difficult; the world still seems to belong to Hobbes, and the sophists and we grow tired of the increasing struggle toward which these words move us. Inwardly we know that the words are true, that we are affected by them like our fellowmen in the past and in the present, and like them we are called upon to act. In action lies the truth of the Idea. Action is reality, the incarnation of the Idea, the realization of moral responsibility, the acceptance of the eternal task. The moral task which is the eternal task is *reality,* that coming together of will and doing in meaning. "Peace," we can say with Cohen, "is the virtue of eternity." We must come to terms with the realization that "everything temporal leads to eternity if it goes on the right road."[22] The moral task is eternal, our work belongs to eternity, the temporality of our thinking and doing is a preparation for eternity. Temporality is not the fullness of acting, we belong to time and time belongs to us, but the end is not in time but in the eternal. "Peace is the sign of eternity and also the watchword for human life, in its individual conduct as well as in the eternity of its historical calling. In this historical eternity the mission of peace of messianic mankind is completed."[23] These were Cohen's last words. They are significant words which the philosophers after Cohen put easily aside. They were no longer Kantians. Such Cohenian idealism did not suit the temper of the times. Peace, "the eternity of its historical calling," is the grand and sharp refusal to any attempt to reduce philosophy to temporality, fate and history. Man has an eternal moral task and responsibility. What is reduced to temporality are phenomena like wanton hatred that distorts the soul and isolates man from community. Man in hatred is man in isolation. His brooding and inordinate self-reflection is madness. Hatred is self-reflection turning to madness. Temporality that is no longer eternity is demonic self-indulgence.

At the end of the "Doctrine of Virtue" in the *Metaphysics of Morals,* Kant asked the question which we all have posed. "What is it in you that can be trusted to enter into combat with all the powers of nature in you and around you and, if they come into conflict with your moral principles, to conquer them?"[24] Kant replied: "And if he takes it to heart, the very incomprehensibility of this self-knowledge must produce an exaltation in his soul which only inspires it the more to keep its duty holy, the more it is assailed."[25] The struggle against wanton hatred is rooted in commitment to the moral principles that are embodied in the Idea of Mankind. Our capacity to hold in check the morality and political consequence of this hatred is doubtful, but it is from this doubt that we gain strength. If there were surety there would be no struggle. Man masters his world not by his command of factual reality but through his reason and its power to impose upon it meaning, reasonable discourse. The problem of peace is not only a political and moral problem; it is in the Kantian sense, an anthropological one. Peace must be able to move the soul, it must have the power to root out the hatred that lives in it without cause and meaning. Hatred is demonic because it is banal. Peace is a moral command, from it philosophy finds its moral justification and task. "Peace is the virtue of eternity," it drives man from the demonic security of temporality, the certainty of fate, and forces him to act as if his doing belongs to the eternal. Human destiny is not limited to what is the moment or to a recapitulation of what has been the past. Man has future and with it comes moral purpose: that unity of Monotheism and Messianism. If these are religious terms, they are nevertheless filled with philosophical meaning. They reveal the eternity that is philosophy.

We have brought into focus the contradiction of peace and hatred. This contradiction makes us aware of the sharp battle between hatred that infects and weakens the soul and peace that is the harmony of the soul of humanity. Man's moral weakness returns him to bestiality; his strength gives him that supreme virtue which is *Sophrosyne,* the harmony of intellectual and moral powers. The philosopher is not a scientist, philosophy is not *a* science, it is *the* science of sciences because it is ultimately concerned with *ends.* Philosophy is teleological. In posing the question of the end, philosophy poses the eternal question. In knowing that temporality is the path to eternity, philosophy belongs to the Idea and the Ideal. It is the way and essence of peace.

In philosophy there is no separation between theory and practice. What is theoretical is already practical and what is practice is derived from theory. The philosopher should be the embodiment of both moments of reality; he must move from one to the other naturally. In him theory and practice are philosophical life. In this life he brings the world of ideas into being. In his hope he creates hope, in his justice, justice, in his compassion, compassion. The philosopher adheres to the words of Albert Schweitzer, he believes that his calling is to be "leader and watchman of reason." This he teaches his fellow man. Need he teach anything else? Perhaps the humility that few are philosophers, that none are wise, and that the others are in search of the meaning of human reality overcomes the illusion that they can be philosophers. He teaches the difficulty of the search, he shows the courage, the pain and the trust it demands. In this he is a being of action, deeply human and efficacious.

Philosophy has the task of proclaiming the events of the human mind. It stands in opposition to the unknown.

7

The Opposition to Kantian Ethics

The interest we take in history or philosophy depends upon the questions we put to ourselves, to our fellowmen and to the world. These questions emerge from our attitudes and perspectives, from our situation and our needs. If we have never believed that religion is the explanation of the universe then we find in it another belief: the condition for man's moral development. The differences of perspective and need give rise to fundamentally distinct outlooks. I remember a text of Léon Brunschvicg which offered some reflections on a book of Vladimir Jankelevitch, *La Nuit* (1942). In his letter to Jankelevitch, Brunschvicg said:

> I give more freely my ears and my heart to the music of the night because I am aware of being the bourgeois in the eyes of those for whom the night is only entertained in the remembrance and hope of the light. We are disposed to think that the day has fear of the night and romanticism takes justifiable pleasure in its triumph over this fear. The danger begins, however, when the same person who no longer has fear of the night begins, like Wagner, to proclaim his fear of the day. It should be shown to him that nocturnal rays are only reflections of diurnal clarity.[1]

Why these reflections of Brunschvicg to begin a paper on compassion, suffering and sympathetic sorrow in Kant and Hermann Cohen, can be easily answered. The ambiance in which the Neo-Kantians worked, and in particular Brunschvicg, Cohen, Cassirer, and Weil is described by Brunschvicg with poetical feeling and depth. Their refusal to be enticed by myth, pessimism, or fate was a victory for their belief in reason. In behalf of reason and reasonableness, of morality and human relationships, they fought the good fight against the forces of obscurantism in ethics, aesthetics and epistemology. The European spirit was the ideal of their struggle for transcendence and universality. The rise of totalitarianism brought their work to a momentary end. We endeavor to carry forth their sense of critique, their devotion to clarity and precision, and their unending struggle to judge reality from the commands and demands of the universal.

Eric Weil spoke of the breakthroughs and breakdowns in history which I would imagine would include philosophy. In the work of Hermann Cohen the problem of ethics was the central concern of his work and in this he achieved a breakthrough. He made it possible for us to comprehend the reality of the *Thou,* to go beyond the *He.* In his last work, *The Religion of Reason,* Cohen established the importance of the feeling of *Mitleid,* i.e., compassion, sympathetic suffering as the foundation of the discovery of the fellowman. If Neo-Kantianism brought philosophy close to science it did so to comprehend the possibilities of reason as the source of human creativity, to give man a rational dignity of which he could easily be deprived by irrational beliefs: the notion of fate and moral and political pessimism. Man's moral and rational dignity is comprehensible only if we ascribe to him feelings that make his fellowman not simply a source of calculated help, but a being for whom he has compassion, whose physical and spiritual suffering he shares with love and respect. Are these feelings arbitrarily motivated by pleasure and pain or do they reflect a sharing of humaneness, a sensitivity for the humanity in every man? The question is difficult but cannot be put aside. Cohen asked the question in the following way: "What difference does it make from the point of view of humanity if I should have to address another example of humanity not merely as He, but expressly and above all as Thou?"[2]

The question of difference belongs also to that of consequence and to the question of how it is possible to move from the He to the Thou? Many discussions have centered on this problem from the works of Ebner, to those of Buber, Marcel and Levinas, but it is in Cohen that the problem takes its fundamental dimensions. In him the struggle is to comprehend why it is absent in Kant's *Metaphysics of Morals* and does not reappear in critiques of Kant until Cohen discovers in Kant the reason for the absence.

The question for Cohen had wider implications since ethics considers every man as an embodiment or symbol of humanity. Every individual has the same intrinsic value. Does the Thou threaten this equality of value or does it add a new dimension to it? Cohen remarked that "should the question arise, however, as to the specific value and distinction of this address that marks out the Thou and seems to endanger the identity of mankind, then it becomes necessary to investigate the particular contribution that the discovery of the Thou makes to the concept of the individual."[3]

The problem is now focused on the peculiar discovery which the Thou makes of the ethical demand for universality. Is this ethical demand adequate to the human condition without the idea and reality of the Thou? Is not every universal concern lacking when it does not yield a valid individualization? We cannot forget that when man thinks the universal he thinks from his individuality and from its needs. Man is always individual and this individuality always has meaning for him.

When Cohen raised the question of how significant the Thou is for ethics he indicated the distinction that Kant had made between love and respect. In the *Metaphysics of Morals* Kant spoke of duties to others and wrote that "when we are speaking of laws of duty (not laws of nature) and among these of laws governing men's external relations with one another, we are considering a moral (intelligible) world where, by analogy with the physical world, *attraction* and *repulsion* bind together rational beings (on earth). The principle of *mutual love* admonishes men constantly to *come nearer* to each other; that of *respect* which they owe each other, to keep themselves at a *distance* from one another."[4]

We are dealing with the fundamental distinction between *Wechselliebe* and *Achtung,* between an obligation which binds myself to others and others to me, and one that binds only myself. In the mutual binding of *Wechselliebe* there arises the sense of community, the foundation of the covenant or agreement in and through which men bind themselves to others. This mutual love that becomes mutual responsibility causes the individual to find falsity in individuality *per se*. Individuality assumes its validity, i.e., its justification in the concern for social, economic and political justice. The community in which social justice is the highest and demanding obligation gives man freedom from his individuality, his I is discovered in his fellowman and embodies its awareness of freedom in societal mutuality. Respect leaves the individual in "social" isolation. The individual realizes in and through himself that distinct separation which alone makes him worthy of being the bearer of the moral law. This aloneness distorts his moral life, it perverts the nature of his humaneness, it reduces his need for his fellowman. As man moves away from this moral isolation he introduces himself to the fellowman with his needs and desires, as he moves from it he seeks to reduce and overcome these needs and desires in societal apathy. He seeks to be the sage rather than the indigent man, he rejects philosophy for wisdom.

Cohen pursued the question of the Thou from another perspective. "Is the He," Cohen asked, "only another example of the I, which is therefore established by the I? Language alone protects us from this mistake, language sets up the Thou before the He. Is the Thou also only another example of the I or is a separate discovery of the Thou necessary, even if I have already become aware of my own I? Perhaps the opposite is the case, that only the Thou, the discovery of the Thou, is able to bring myself to the discovery of I to the discovery of the ethical knowledge of my I?"[5]

These interrogations are of vital interest to Cohen. The most meaningful concern belongs to the discovery of man as fellowman. The question is no longer how ethics is possible, but what is the foundation of practical ethics in which the possibility of its foundation can be discovered. In other words, in the circular movement of thought the first question, that of the possibility of the practical reason should make possible practical morality, but in fact the realization of the foundation of practical morality in man as fellowman raises the possibility of the theoretical foundation of ethics. From the theoretical to the practical question the movement of thought shows how inseparable are these questions. In Kant we find no interrogations about man as fellowman. Kant's concern is primarily that of Luther's: the freedom of a Christian man. Cohen's concern belongs to that of Ezekiel, Isaiah, Jeremiah; this concern is inseparable from the community, from a covenant which, in time, discovers and links man to man, to higher and deeper levels of societal responsibility and mutuality. The Thou for Cohen makes possible the I because community precedes individuality and social justice is more significant than the human divine relationship. The recognition and obligation toward the injustices born in human poverty is more significant for Cohen as the creation of a collective human response than of an individual need to observe and become sensitive to man's suffering. The Idea of mankind is a collective responsibility and therefore must be organized to respond societally. This in no way divorces the individual from responsibility, but it reveals the fact that individuality has meaning only as mutuality, as societal activity, as collective responsibility.

A pertinent and serious question emerges from all the previous interrogations. Cohen has pointed the way to an overcoming of Kant's ethics. His interrogations have led him to the realization that without the concept of the fellowman there can be no practical morality, no sense of community. We remain with abstract universality and each man is judged to be the embodiment of the ethical command which says: Act as if.... We have a world of modes, a community of disembodied souls all in communication with a moral law or substance. Each mode assumes to have the authority of the divine command. The nature of time and space are no longer the realms in which man decides to act or refrain from action, where the problem of right and wrong evokes within him a conscience that demands that he take responsibility for what he does, that he realize his dependence upon his fellowman, the community and the world. The question which we referred to is in reality two: "Is it within the competence of the ethical method to bring about the discovery of the Thou? In accordance with the concept of man, as the man of humanity, is ethics able to enter into classification of the individual?"[6]

Where are we heading with these questions if not away from ethics that has, as its highest idea, totality. We move toward the reality of the individual, of mutuality and plurality? The individual can be comprehended as fellowman and not simply as a mode of totality. Cohen would say that "the Thou introduces a new problem into the concept of man which, however, still reaches its completion — as individual also — in the concept of humanity."[7]

Cautiously Cohen introduced the new concept. He had spoken of it in *The Concept of Religion in the System of Philosophy* (1915). Now it comes forth fully as the problem of the Thou with radical implications for ethics, for religion and for a humanism that is no longer an abstract universality and totality. Cohen emerges as Kant's severest opponent.

Our concern is to discover how the Thou, as a moral concept, reveals the I. The Thou and I are neither poetic nor metaphysical concepts. They are rooted in a fundamental mutual human experience which is forever realizing the depths of man's moral nature. Human suffering is a quality of life which we share with all men. We are not indifferent to suffering; we discover ourselves in it. Suffering links the body to the spirit. In suffering man overcomes the dichotomy of body and soul if ever such a dichotomy existed outside of thought. Cohen remarked that morally "self consciousness should not be indifferent to one's own physical suffering"[8] nor should man be indifferent to the pain of fellowman. If we should not be indifferent then the pain of the other forces us to realize that He has become a Thou. Suffering is the bond that joins us to our fellow being; it awakens in us the feeling that it is the inescapable fate of all men. This is not to be taken as a tragic and metaphysical destiny to be accepted with apathy and sacred indifference. This removes us to a tranquil isolation where we strive for a saintliness that forcefully divides us from our fellowman and takes from us the need and the desire to alleviate his suffering and that of society.

Suffering and pain do not only belong to the individual situation. The problem is not resolved in my identification with this or that person's pain. The individual situation necessitates a deeper moral attitude. Suffering becomes *the* orientation in the moral world. Cohen remarked that "it is only narrow-mindedness that could make me indifferent to suffering, and it is only ignorance of the specific worth of man that, guided by erroneous metaphysics, degrades compassion to a reflex action."[9]

Denying this indifference, a Kantian indifference, Cohen made it possible for philosophy to discover in compassion the universal basis of the idea of mankind, to find in poverty, political and social injustice, not simply momentary distorted conditions, but those circumstances by which each man finds within himself the meaning of his humanity, the movement from the I to the fellowman. My capacity for compassion is the source of my dignity and worthiness for happiness. Whatever social doctrine man accepts the dignity of man is its core, but this dignity is discovered in mutuality in the realization of the self as the societal self. Not in the falsity of obsolete individuality do we find the foundation of ethics, but in the fellowman that we should find in ourselves.

Kant mentioned that sympathetic joy and sorrow, *Mitfreude und*

Mitleid, "are really sensuous feelings of a pleasure and pain (which should therefore be called aesthetic) at another's state of happiness or sadness (shared feeling, feeling participated in). Nature has already implanted in man the susceptibility for these feelings."[10]

Cohen refuse to allow *Mitleid* to become a mere "reflex action." The example that Kant provided and which he believed showed a "noble cast of mind" was that of the Stoic's sage who said: "I want a friend not that he might help me in poverty, sickness, imprisonment, etc., but rather that I might stand by him and rescue a man. But the same sage, when he could not save his friend, said to himself: what is it to me? In other words, he repudiated imparted suffering."[11]

Suffering, Kant implies, is an evil and there is little virtue in its perpetuation, i.e., in "sympathetic sadness, *Mitleid.*" Kant went on to say that "this would also be an insulting kind of beneficence, since it expresses benevolence with regard to the unworthy, *den Unwuerdigen,* pity, *Barmherzigkeit,* which has no place in men's relations with one another...."[12]

We read these observations with sad astonishment. They reflect an attitude that moves in a diametrically opposite direction from that of Cohen. He sought, through what he believed to be man's religious and moral responsibility, for social justice, to reveal not merely man's moral autonomy but his realization of his societal responsibility, and for the creation of the fellowman from the I. In the fellowman, in community with him, in his suffering and pain, in his poverty and inequalities, man reveals the fact that he becomes a man not through birth, but through social consciousness. The rejecting of the idealization of the self is the path to humaneness and to the realization of mutuality and plurality. These ideas are not the ideas of the sage. These are discovered in *Mitleid,* in compassion and sympathetic suffering. They bind the humanity in each of us to the other, i.e., to the emerging fellowman as well as to the emerging I which is the source of both intellectual and moral awareness.

If in compassion man discovers in himself his fellowman, and with a deepened sensitivity for social inequalities he becomes more aware of the mutuality of human relationships, and the dependence of man upon man for action and decision in human affairs, then we can affirm that the moral law emerges from a recognition of humanity in the growing consciousness of suffering as the veritable social reality. Cohen then raised the following question: "If interest in suffering and compassion now is recognized as an ethical interest distinct from a theoretical explanation of the world, and therefore distinct also from all alleged metaphysics, then the questions arise: What does ethical practice gain? Of what method can it take possession in order to solve the fundamental riddle of ethics?"[13]

The fundamental concern of ethics is totality and universality, but man's fundamental interest is the alleviation of his physical and spiritual suffering, a reality he shares with all men and in which he discovers the moral self. Man developed ethics from a need to comprehend the idea of totality. This totality is man's and he comprehends it as he does universality in terms of what meaning it has for him. In a similar way, man speaks of his individual situation and his concern for his fellowman. Man always speaks from the perspective of meaning. In fact, man needs to refer every experience to his own need for sense and purpose. Even when man introduces religion he does this to enhance the meaning he had previously discovered in his ethical speculations. Cohen's opposition to the problem of suffering from the perspective of tragedy or theodicy is posited in his conviction that only as a moral problem does man assume the obligation to comprehend suffering. He assumes the need for collective responsibility to lessen the discriminatory, the economic inequities and political aberrations that bring with them the loss of personal freedom and dignity. The comprehension of suffering leads not only to practical action but to the discovery of the moral self, to the I and to the Thou.

From these insights into the relationship between the universal and particular perspectives Cohen found himself in radical contradiction to Kant's Stoicism and Spinozism. Cohen said that "if through suffering and compassion the Thou in man is discovered, then the I may appear liberated from the shadow of selfishness. . . . To have compassion with one's own suffering does not have to be simply overt and fruitless sentimentality."[14]

Physical suffering and pain is no cause for embarrassment and isolation. To be aware and sympathetic with another's physical pain is the most intimate and profound relationship we can have with another. It is felt as that powerful feeling we call love. Our cry of embarrassment comes forth when we feel the inadequacy in our self to be compassionate. We are troubled by our distance and non-concern, and by the ease with which we forget and move quickly to other more pleasant activities. Not only does the need of our fellowmen require our concern, but we are now able to understand Cohen when he said that "Humanity requires consideration for one's own suffering." Our individuality has its truth in its humanity. We are individual with a universal need. The human situation is distorted when either individuality or universality command its exclusive loyalty. The body is not subject to the soul nor is the soul subject to the body. Their truth is in their mutuality, i.e., their dependency.

Kant, who had no idea of the fellowman, of the Thou, speaks cryptically of the meaning of his suffering for us. He wrote that "when another person suffers and, although I cannot help him, I let myself be infected by his sorrow (by means of my imagination), then the two of us suffer, though the evil actually (in nature) affects the one."[15]

The working of these observations gives the impression that although the pain of another does affect me, I must make sure that the pain does not touch me too deeply. I feel as if I am before a diseased individual and my good sense tells me to show sympathy, but learn distance. We are back to Kant's preference for respect over love, for the Stoic and the nobility of his apathy, for the noble character of Spinoza and of the soul over the body. This heritage that gave preference to spirit over the body had a devastating societal and moral consequence. European culture had to wait until the religious creeds which perpetuated their low esteem of the body were finally tempered and man's physical life and its political and social affects restored to him the value and meaning of physical life. Cohen would allow no distinction to be made between our obligation to our physical suffering and to that of the soul. "Corporeality belongs to the soul of the individual and the soul is neglected when the affliction of the body is neglected."[16]

This is demanded not only by our individuality but also by our humanity. The physical poverty and its consequent hunger and disease which we observe about us may leave us helpless, but in a poignant way the poor, the sick, and the helpless are part of our humanity, and although we can turn from them, dismiss their condition, or place their fate in the hands of God, these are feelings for our fellow human beings that remind us then that their pain can be ours, that all men suffer and no man is free of pain.

Kant spoke of an "indirect duty" to cultivate our sympathetic natural feelings, i.e., not to avoid the sick and the unfortunate. What we do with this cultivation is hard to grasp. Do we become better human beings? Do we take pride in our ability to have sympathetic feelings, or knowing that we have them, do we now have the capacity to stand apart and be satisfied with the moral quality of our sensitivities? The feeling never escapes us that Kant preferred the sacred distance of the sage, and that the tribulations and woes of others seem to have been the consequence of the divine decree. Kant told us that it was our duty: "not to avoid places where we shall find the poor who lack the most basic essentials, but rather to seek them out, not to shun sick-rooms and debtors' prisons in order to avoid the painful sympathetic feelings that we cannot guard against."[17]

The text reads like the advice given to a man who should cultivate his capacity to see the evils of life, face their harshness and be able to walk away from them stronger and more convinced of his own moral worth, that he is morally enhanced because he has strengthened a natural inclination without having to resort to the notion of a duty. The man has now a heightened and enhanced sense of his ability to be affected by the senses, but not controlled by them. He is a philosopher-sage whose moral autonomy allows him to dominate all forms of life without being molested by them. He has developed a moral indifference that protects him from sharing in the evils which afflict both man and the world. This benevolence which we exercise toward the unfortunate has a singular purpose, "to present the world in its full perfection as a beautiful moral whole even if we do not take into account the advantages it brings (in the way of happiness)."[18]

Cohen warned us against the dangers that faced our discovery of the Thou when we attempt to comprehend the nature of the misfortune of others. The woes of man are not theoretical questions nor can the origin of evil be allowed to become a theoretical question. Asking the Why of these questions leads to the following considerations: If the theoretical dominates then I face the Thou, my fellowman as "a carrier of evil, and, thus, the barely discovered Thou would at once be lost again."[19]

The theoretical questions yield to practical moral questions. I am not concerned with the origin of evil nor with man's woes as possible exemplifications of destiny or divine suffering. My concern is the alleviation of the inequalities and their social disorientations. I am concerned with a communal and national will and with activities that reveal to me how the other man becomes a fellowman. I am concerned with a sensitivity to social and political arbitrariness and distortion. The concern for programs of reform are of greater importance than the cultivation of my own natural proclivity for sympathetic feelings. I am concerned with my sense of social responsibility. Cohen could not escape the demands for social responsibility. Cohen could not escape the demands for social justice which he learned from the prophets. Kant could not escape the idea of the freedom of the Christian man which he learned from Luther and the Pietists. Cohen was Kantian in ethics but with limits. He could bring to Kant's ethics new directions, but these came slowly and when they finally appeared they were a "breakthrough" which we are only now beginning to comprehend as we read his final book with care and insight. Neither Cassirer, nor Weil, nor Brunschvicg followed the depths of Cohen's innovations in ethics. They simply did not read him. They kept closely to the paths of epistemology. Others, like Rosenzweig, Buber, Levinas, went to the poetic, the religious and the mystical. They were philosophers of the person. They dramatized their peculiar experiences.

There is little doubt that Cohen's breakthrough in the realm of ethics did not fully take place in either his book on *Kant's Foundation of Ethics* or in his *Ethics of Pure Reason.* Cohen always hinted at his discovery, but only in his last work does there emerge with clarity and preciseness the idea of man as fellowman. It was not easy to shed the weight of Idealism even in ethics. The "Discovery of Man as Fellowman" is a unique chapter of his last book; ethical idealism loses its dominance. There he stated with clarity that "the concept of the fellowman conceals a correlation of its own, namely, that of man and man," not of one man alongside of man, of a *Nebenmensch,* but of fellowman, a *Mitmensch.* The love of man to man is not rooted in subjective satisfaction, but finds its law in the humanity that lives in man, or if we want to express it religiously, we speak of the divine spirit that lives in him. We love that spirit of God that every man bears in him and our link to him in and through it. This love has a more practical reality. In creating the man who is unknown and indifferent to me into a fellowman, a radical innovation must occur. I must have a more direct and practical relationship with this other man. His condition awakens in me concern and distress, his misfortunes disturb my indifference. I am stirred by them; I feel a sense of refusal and rejection. I declare that it is unjust that people hunger, that children have improper medical attention and care, that governments restrict basic freedoms and that human rights are arbitrarily violated. I am conscious of injustice only if it exists. I would have no moral concerns without injustice. When they can be overlooked I am indifferent. In a world of justice I would be morally neutral. In the injury, the woe, the pain, my conscience awakens. Without injustice men would be a-moral. Without imperfection I would no longer know my conscience.

Cohen's insight was to begin the discussion of the problem of the Thou with poverty. This was innovative and deeply suggestive. Although he often buries the issue in others, the careful reader knows when the analysis begins again. *"Poverty,"* Cohen said, *"becomes the main representation of human misfortune.* Thereby physical ill in general becomes moral ill."[20]

Moral ill must be divorced from paralyzing guilt. It is a condition that afflicts each of us who wants to find comfort in reducing moral problems to metaphysical ones. They are moral as long as we are willing to believe that our actions and decisions count in a world that is not adverse or destructive of them. Cohen's fundamental concern was to show that "suffering only reaches ethical precision as social suffering. Whoever explains poverty as the suffering of mankind, creates ethics or, if not philosophical ethics, yet still religion with its share of reason. Only the religion of reason is moral religion, and only moral religion is truthful and true religion, *wahrhaftige und wahre Religion.*"[21]

Cohen has withdrawn the problem of practical ethics from the maxim yielding universal laws to the reality of social injustices. Ethics has passed from the realm of maxims, from totality and universality to that of concrete social and political action. Cohen joined these problems to those of purpose. He had earlier remarked that "purpose becomes the new guiding concept of knowledge and at the same time a new concept of the content of the spirit. And with the notion of purpose the concept of correlation moves from the realm of theoretical knowledge into the realm of the ethical."[22] In the question of purpose lies man's power of action and decision. Man cannot escape questioning the purpose of his life.

When man confronts the wrongs and misfortunes of social, economic and political systems the questions he puts to himself, his fellowman and his community deal with the means for changes and the purposes that are embodied in human responsibility and action. Moral life may be theoretically contemplated. We can say with Kant that "I want every other man to be benevolent to me; hence I should also be benevolent to every other man."[23]

We find these statements useful and necessary but they have little significance when we face problems that need to be resolved and are not casuistries. We know that those who want to avoid practical morality seek theoretical perfection. Their ideal is the sage. Man finds pleasure in being a sage. He likes the idea of indifference and takes pride in rejecting as meaningless the everyday life of man in time and space. Yet neither he nor anyone else escapes this daily life. In it we make our most important decisions. In it we face man's inadequacies, moral indifferences and cruelties, but there exists the possibilities for us to act and risk our well-being. In this world we learn what it is to exercise courage or cowardice, to be just or deceptive, to have benevolence or indifference. In the theoretical world where we are separated from the real quality of time and space these attitudes and risks are of theoretical importance. Cohen knew well — he spoke of the issues of his own age — that moral survival meant opposition to racism, sexual perversity, pessimism. It meant positive action: helping indigent immigrants, support of education and the contribution of monies to meaningful welfare programs. Cohen, the philosopher, the Idealist, was also a man who had a sensitivity for human suffering and pain. Not even religion could escape the fact that the correlation of God and man was sensible only when built on the social relationships of man to man. The ethical socialism of Cohen brought together the need for man's dignity and the need to abolish his poverty.

Suffering comes forth not only from the voice of Medea, Phaedra and Oedipus, it belongs to an economic reality, to a fearsome human condition: the poverty that distorts and cripples the human spirit. This suffering is a consciousness which determines all our other human concerns. "The sufferings of poverty must always remain the problem: the religious problem, but not the metaphysical one." We wonder about the sources of Cohen's profound sense of misfortune and we must not forget the name of Friedrich Albert Lange, the man who brought him to Marburg and whose successor he became in the chair of philosophy. Lange had this sense of social responsibility, this prophetic, biblical, permeation with man's obligation to man as fellowman. He accepted the fact that man becomes truly unique when he is concerned with social justice, with the other as social brother. The consciousness reached its deepest level when we became aware that knowledge and aesthetics were not enough and that man had to participate in his society. Cohen's most striking insight, the power that created his breakthrough was his realization that *"only social suffering is spiritual suffering."* All the complexities of consciousness, including knowledge, is affected by it, and takes part in it. This is the profound meaning of social suffering: that "the entire consciousness of culture is implicated in it." I write these lines and I think of Cohen's insight, the power and the awe evoked by these observations, and I think of a commentary. I have none. The words are to be read again and again. In the reading I know I will find clarification. The implications of Cohen's thought are yet to be realized, but when we comprehend them together with Kant's we grasp the radical changes he brought about.

Cohen was now able to say that "the poor man typifies man in general.... For even if I had no heat in my body, my education alone would have brought me to the insight that the great majority of men cannot be isolated from me, and that I myself am nothing if I do not make myself a part of them."[24]

So deeply has compassion become a part of Cohen's ethics that we realize that it is its deepest revelation and manifestation. To understand its impact and its significance, Fritz Kaufmann has called our attention to a serious comparison. Karl Jaspers, whose philosophy is one of the great tributes of reason to the European spirit, in its darkest hours, never spoke of compassion. Kaufmann remarked that there is little evidence of it in Jaspers' writing. He went on to say that there "is compassion in all human love, since there is suffering in all human beings. It is through compassion, according to Cohen, that the 'other' being becomes my 'fellow' being with whom I bear and for whom I live. This is religious socialism which is not contrary, but complementary, to religious individualism."[26]

The absence of compassion is evident not only in the work of Karl Jaspers but also in that of Cassirer, Husserl, Brunschvicg *inter alia*. Nietzsche fought against compassion, but his attitude is more comprehensible assuming the nature of his philosophy of man. Why, we may ask, was this true among the Neo-Kantians? Had the European spirit become so deeply involved in epistemological problems that it failed utterly to grasp the meaning of ethical plurality and mutuality or had the prophetic tradition lost all meaning? Did the exclusivity of the epistemological question weaken the ethical?

Cohen's ethics became the most radical confrontation with the Stoical tradition of apathy in Western culture. He opposed social suffering which he distinguished from individual physical suffering to the exclusivity of individuality. Social suffering afflicts the majority of men is "the qualitative evidence of the low level of the culture." This critique of society showed that where society could attain a high level of technological and theoretical accomplishment, and ignored or gave little attention to social justice, that society has failed in humaneness and has violated the dignity and humanity of its members. In fact from the perspective of a moral society where there is consciousness of human misfortune and compassion, there is individuality as social responsibility. Without this sense we fall in line with Nietzsche and shake our heads in agreement when he tells us that those who desire "to serve mankind as a physician *in any sense whatever* will have to be very much on his guard against that sensation (Mitleid) — it will paralyze him at every decisive moment and apply a ligature to his knowledge and his subtle helpful hand."[27]

Cohen maintained that community was reciprocal action, *"Die Gemeinschaft ist Wechselwirkung."*[28]

Social suffering affects not merely the intellect but more powerfully and decidedly it affects the heart. Cohen refused to retreat into the legacy of, and rejected the individual as the exclusive source of reality. He repeated the notion that suffering was social suffering and maintained the assumption that "an understanding of it cannot be furthered by any kind of insight that concerns only the individual."[29]

It is, however, the individual who has feelings, is conscious of them, who is confronted with misfortune and suffering, whose physical pain makes him sympathetic to all pain and its alleviation. Is it only the perspective and situation of the individual in the concreteness of his existence that we discover conscience and the need for the fellowman? If the insistence of Cohen is upon the word *only* he is right to reject the individual expression as the objective experience although man is the one who thinks both the practical and the theoretical. He is not a disembodied soul but the being who thinks and acts, who feels, loves and gives respect. Feelings, however, can be replaced by indifference. Man, who can be indifferent, and can be moved by great feeling knows the difference between them. The same man embodies both qualities within himself. Culture depends upon which of these he is moved to develop. How far is he capable of going from individuality to community, from self to societal concern, from *Nebenmensch* to *Mitmensch*?

Cohen severely condemns the notion that *Mitleid* or compassion is nothing other than an elemental common feeling like hunger and ease, like pleasure, aversion and pain, like pride and envy, in short, like passion in general. Kant, in the *Metaphysics of Morals*, said that *Mitleid* like *Mitfreude* were sensuous feelings, *sinnliche Gefuehle*. Was the image of Kant beyond critique or did Cohen not contemplate the extent of the change he had initiated when he made compassion the source of the idea of fellowman, of the Thou, and the love of neighbor dependent upon God's creation of man, the realization in him of the likeness of God. In this all men are sons of Noah before they are sons of Abraham. "But before he is a son of Abraham and a son of Noah," Cohen reminded us, "the Israelite, just as every man, is God's creature and is created in his image."[30]

The idea of the human community, of mutuality and of responsibility for the neighbor becomes the bond which creates in each man a sense of dependence and compassion for the other. The Thou which I find in every being is the image of God. This is the humanity that makes it possible for man to comprehend the meaning of the idea of humanity as universality and the universal. Cohen comprehended this universality in the individual. He said that compassion "unveils the mystery of the individual, the *principium individuationis*: I am always only myself and as many men as I seem to see, yet they are always only myself."[31]

Compassion brings me close to man. In it I find the feeling and consciousness from which the universal emerges and identifies all that is human.

The question which can now be raised is whether "I myself do exist before the fellowman is discovered." I know that the fellowman is not the next man, the *Nebenmensch* or the *Gegenmensch*. The fellowman is revealed in compassion. Without compassion the fellowman, the Mitmensch remains the abstract other, a mode of an ethical substance that embodies a modicum of reason and about whom I can speak with rational terminology that sounds like the wording of a geometric theorem. In the Thou I find the I. In the I the fellowman is discovered. He is not there like the man next to, or facing me, an indifferent being for whom I have only abstract consideration and for whom my I is only an indifferent self. I can only act toward a Thou, a Being whose humanity has become meaningful to men and toward whom I believe that what I do or do not do has significance and efficacy. The discovery of the Thou is a social reality. The problem is not the notoriously famous I and Thou relationship, but the realization that the Thou originates in the sensitivity of poverty, in community, in the reciprocal effects which man has upon man. In the community compassion reveals the fellowman. It reveals the nature of social responsibility. At the deepest levels it reveals to me the quality of my I. I am amoral to the degree that the woes and welfare of my fellow being causes me to act in behalf of them, to feel compassion for their sufferings and to share the joys of their joy. The I is the consequence of my social involvement. The fellowman is a consequence of the same involvement. We grow and develop into these realities. The potentiality for them is given but this does not assure any man of their actuality. In the world about us we face the violence that arises from the loss of universality. This violence is the startling expression of a community where indifference becomes crime and where the moral self has remained obscure and suppressed. In indifference there is no moral self.

Our final remarks concern Cohen's comprehension of prophetic ethics. No force and feeling was more fundamental for his overcoming of the limitations and inadequacies of Kant's ethics than the ethical feelings of the prophets. About them he said:

> Their problem is religious monotheism, the correlation of man and God. And this correlation is intertwined with the correlation between man and man. The first, between man and God may seem to be merely theoretical; the other, however, between man and man is immediately practical. And the fellowman belongs to this second correlation. Therefore, the prophet cannot allow any doubt to direct him from the problem: how the fellowman is to originate is to originate out of pity (Mitleid) for the poor man.[32]

The prophet also brought trust in the future. The fellowman, like the I, belongs not only to the present but also to the future. The future is the hope that we can create an ethical society where compassion will be the serious factor. The feeling is the hope, the foundation of the belief of reason which makes those who are committed to it philosophers and not sages. We must know that our decisions and actions are meaningful and that they will help to decrease the inequalities and sufferings that men place upon others. We need to believe that there is a growing sense of humanity and humaneness in the world community. Cohen once remarked that we have only begun to be religious. We could modify the remark and say that we have only begun to be moral, that we are just emerging in our history with an increased sense of conscience. To the question of whether we are our brother's keeper: the affirmation has just begun to be part of man's consciousness. The universal in the Idea has grasped few of us but we believe there is a future and it is not necessarily antithetical to our belief in the Idea of Humanity. Universality is an abstraction, but it is also the powerful belief in reason.

Cohen's ethics is a breakthrough and I believe that these remarks have indicated the direction and nature of it. Much more of the breakthrough has yet to be revealed. In these revelations, which belong to the future, I find the realization of the humanity that embraces all men, even in the deepest perversions. Cohen brought the prophets to Kant. They were needed to counter his dependence upon the nobility of the Sage and the wisdom that deafened the voice of philosophy. Cohen heard the prophetic call for social justice. He heard it more concretely than the ethical apathy of indifference.

8

The Aesthetic Consciousness and the *Religion of Reason*

Hermann Cohen's massive work *Ästhetik des reinen Gefühls* has the rare distinction of remaining undisturbed on the library shelf, sharing with his other significant books the tranquility of not being opened. Different from his logic or his ethics, the aesthetics is even less cited than the other two parts of Cohen's philosophical system.

A book that is not read is a challenge to the courageous who are willing to read at least some of its hundreds of pages. There is much to be learned from its contents, and it rewards the efforts of those who make them. The book, was published in 1912, the year Cohen left Marburg to teach for six years at a Jewish institute in Berlin. This study has a simple purpose. It does not aim at a review of the aesthetics, for that would be impossible. The attempt is made to comprehend the relationship between the pure feeling and what Cohen has called the peculiarity of religion. He believed that logic and ethics were bases for religion, but less often does he mention the significance of aesthetics. However, at the end of his *Religion of Reason out of the Sources of Judaism* he refers to the *Aesthetics*. He states:

> In the *Aesthetics of Pure Feeling* I have tried to show that the feeling of being moved furnishes a proof of the aesthetic consciousness. However, this view does not contradict our attempt at this time to claim the feeling of being moved for the religious consciousness in its virtuous way of peace. For the religious consciousness uses the aesthetic consciousness as

amply as the ethical consciousness, and there is no reason for the religious consciousness to claim its own originality in the feeling of being moved. The feeling is the love for the nature of man which, expressed in its pureness, shines forth in the countenance of man where it reflects the splendor of this feeling of being moved.[1]

Cohen speaks of the nature of man as the embodiment of his dignity, and the love for man becomes the self-esteem of humanity in man, *das Selbstgefühl der Menschheit im Menschen*.[2] To be affected by the humanity in man, to develop a sensitivity to and belief in the good, necessitates a cultivation of feeling. Yet, we know that this feeling is an original component of consciousness and deeply related to the ethical from which it proceeds, but in which it is not created. The pureness of each moment of consciousness, knowledge, will, and feeling belongs to the continuous self-realization of its autonomous being. In relation to aesthetics, Cohen says that "all artistic creation is an unceasing return to the original feeling, *Urgefühls,* of the individual."[3] The self is therefore never given, i.e., it is never finished. The self is always becoming, always bringing forth from itself, the self of feeling, *das Selbst des Gefühls.* When we think these abstractions, there is a despair which makes us want to resign from them, but we know that they are the consequence of thought and embody the development of the history of man's most precious speculations.

The aesthetic moment of consciousness is objectified in a particular, unique, and closed world, "but this closed world in all its limits is only the particular self. If this self is not the creation of the longing, if it should be valued as pure productivity, then this is the triumph of aesthetics, the confirmation that it is productivity. Aesthetics achieves this triumph through the fact that it has determined the independence of the aesthetic consciousness as feeling."[4] The productivity of the aesthetic consciousness in all forms of art, from poetry to architecture makes us more aware that in us there is an original feeling, an original movement, the realization of an original consciousness which comes forth in movement and feeling, in the love for the nature of man. The aesthetic feeling surpasses every form of manifestation; it is the love of man's self, the feeling of self, the highest realization of what is possible for man's nature. This is achieved not in knowing or in willing, but only in art.

> Thus the self is independent of content, wins its independence not as freedom, this remains a moral good, but as purity.... The original form of humanity comes forth in the genuine work of art, the original form which reveals not only man's spirit and morality, but both only as the nature of man, as the man of nature, as the soul of man in its body, i.e., in its form, *Gestalt*. It is this productive love which sees the form in man's body, bringing to actuality soul and body, the nature of man. This union of body and soul is the form of man, is the work of the self and the product of the self.[5]

Art seeks to embody feeling in the object, to form and structure, in poetry, painting, sculpture, the love of the nature of man, gathering together in limits what is always transcending and transfiguring these same limits, but discovering in them the means to join together the form of body and soul. In the aesthetic object man unifies in form what is scattered and lost in unrealized and undeveloped individuality. In pureness of feeling the oneness of creation is recaptured and grasped in form. Man learns to comprehend humanity in the individual, to embrace it in sounds and words, to see it in forms and structures, to hear it in tones, to will it in the ideal, to think it in the spontaneity and autonomy of thought. The aesthetic in all its variety reveals that original movement which is the consciousness of pure feeling. We are, as men, moved because the reality of humanity, the pureness of feeling, precede the individual awareness of the oneness of the moment of consciousness. "Nowhere," says Cohen, "is material such a limitation for the spirit as is the material of art. The artist belongs to his material, to this material he must join his love, to this material he must devote himself in order to bring forth his self. With this devotion to the material he finds total submission to the nature of man."[6] Here, in submission to the nature of man, the artist, i.e., every man who is capable of realizing in a particular form the universal, achieves that harmony of mind and body which ethics expresses as task, *Aufgabe*, and knowledge as origin, *das Ursprung*. The work of art refuses to separate matter and form, mind and body. Love, as pure feeling, as the love of the nature of man, embraces nature as well as man, but man remains at the center. "There is no aesthetic nature without man at the center."[7] The love of man implies the dignity of man. It is this dignity which necessitates love.

The aesthetic nature of man is an abstraction. This Cohen admits when he compares this abstraction to the religious. We speak of religious feeling, i.e., the longing for transcendence, the feeling of incomparable dependence. Where art flourishes, the love of man is dominant, the man of nature, the nature of man. Here we bypass the individual; the type is significant. Purity of feeling belongs to the abstract. Yet, in this abstraction man can be awakened to individuality; cultivating his sensitivities and feelings, moved by the delicacy and preciosity of love in feeling and acts. Man now has the possibility to comprehend this love in concrete forms of correlation between himself and God. The God to whom he turns he discovers to be the God who was always with him in knowledge, morality, and feeling. Religion is not a new world of feelings, but an added dimension of consciousness. "A creation which would be limited to the form of man would not be possible for religious feeling. In it man is never alone for himself but always in covenant with God."[8] The dignity of man, man's original worth, *Urwert,* is the source of that original movement, it is source in such a way that it stirs, but doesn't create, its presence is already movement. *Urwert, Urbewegung, Urbewusstsein* are all expression which attempt to reveal to us the autonomy of the aesthetic consciousness which we now must comprehend in contrast to religious dependence. Contrast doesn't imply exclusion, but differentiation. What is so meaningful in Cohen's System is the independence and yet mutual dependence of all the moments of consciousness and the peculiarity which religion has in its relationship to them. Religion comprehends what man has already grasped, but this comprehension is not a mere sum of already-known realities; it is a unique restructuring of them. The uniqueness belongs to the correlation between man and God. The religious consciousness cannot conceive of man without God, nor God without man. Religious correlation is born is suffering and compassion, in that distinct and individual existence which links man to his particular human situation, to its inadequacy and pain, its indigency and anxiety. Here it is clearly differentiated from the aesthetic which belongs to the love of the nature of man, to man in the abstract. Art is dependent upon this love which is the genuine feeling, the productive feeling on the aesthetic consciousness. Cohen makes the distinction clear: "The aesthetic feeling has its distinct creative power. Religious compassion does away with all imagery; it renounces it. Its form is the living essence of the human soul, i.e., man not as a type, not as a concept of the multiple nor of the total, but of the individual who is not coordinated with God but who stands in correlation with Him."[9] The distinction is clear, but its clarity is derived from the distinct nature of the aesthetic. What we mean by this is that the *Eigenart* of religion is prepared for in the aesthetic, as well as in the ethical consciousness. The love of the nature of man, of man's nature, is the precise designation of feeling, the pure feeling, the feeling of completeness. Here in this love, in this feeling, the preparation is made for the suffering and compassion which have their source in the religious, in what man experiences in the anxiety of existence, in what it means to stand before God. This standing before God is the new element which is not in the aesthetic, shown in the work of art, in the love that is pure feeling. The longing for God is in the compassion and suffering which man discovers in relationship with his fellow man. The aesthetic consciousness fails to discover the "Other," in this it remains a type; it relates, but not in co-relationship.

Cohen's works show dynamic development. In 1912 he completed his massive work on aesthetics; three years later he undertook another grandiose effort to limit the scope of the aesthetic experience, attempting to comprehend it from the nature of the religious. Every limitation reflects a methodological need to show its limits and the necessity to find in the other moments the required fulfillment. The peculiarity of religion makes it possible to grasp the ethical and the aesthetic from a perspective which defines and narrows their claim to exclusivity. The problem of love from the religious perspective makes it possible to comprehend the limits of aesthetic love, and to come to terms with other aspects of love. Love is not self-evident. "Love is a new concept of religion, which is not identical with sexual love, nor with eros, nor therefore with the aesthetic either."[10] When we speak of love, many relationships are implied; we think of man's love for God, for God's love of man, for man's love of man. "Man," Cohen remarked, "is the original model, *Urmodell,* of art. The love for man is the original feeling of artistic creation and pleasure."[11] The wonder and glory of man in all his misery and degeneration are the sources of great poetic imagination, the creative imagination which is inspired by man's nature and is the original power, *Urkraft,* of productivity. "Feeling, love for man, is the original power, but the pure feeling is productivity. This productivity becomes more actual in the image of man which is the body of his soul."[12] Yet, there is another dimension to this problem of love. Here in the pure feeling, in that love of man's nature, religion now speaks of the "sufferings of love.," Love and suffering are correlated. "Das Leiden des Menschen ist der Charakter des Individuums."[13] In this simple but powerful statement, Cohen now embodies the love for man in a new comprehension of man's individuality: man's suffering is the characteristic of his individuality. "Not only does the body suffer and hunger in poverty, but the entire man is torn out of the equilibrium of his culture. ... If you wish to know what man is, then get to know his suffering. ... And therefore everything, man himself, begins with social love, with this social pity for the poverty-stricken. Thus it is established beyond doubt that love, as religious love, begins with the love of man."[14]

Is this a radical change? We can answer in the affirmative as well as in the negative. Cohen's philosophy of religion is deeply rooted in the relationships which men must and should establish among themselves. These societal responsibilities precede their comprehension of their relationships to God or God's relationship to them. The feeling for the human, for what Cohen called the nature of man, becomes the necessary preparation for the realization of the human in the concrete situations of suffering and poverty. Sensitivity to injustice, violence, and arbitrariness is the foundation of all relationships. "Love first teaches man to love man. First it teaches man to recognize in poverty the suffering of man. First it teaches, therefore, in correspondence with his social insight into suffering, the kindling in man of the primeval feeling of pity. First it teaches, therefore, the establishment in pity of the true meaning of religious love, and the strict distinction of this true love ... from the aesthetic pleasure, which is interwoven with it. First it teaches, therefore, the discovery in the next man of the fellow man, *im Mitmenschen den Menschen zu entdecken.*"[15] No matter how deeply we study the history of thought in the nineteenth century, it would be difficult to discover a philosopher whose ethical and religious commitment was so deeply sensitive to the social and economic conditions of his fellow man, and who necessitated those who read him seriously, to comprehend philosophy not only as speculation, but as the intimate involvement in the human condition. Compassion or pity, suffering and poverty were not realities which the philosopher could with impunity avoid or ignore; they were the concerns with which a meaningful relationship to God began and developed. The idea of humanity, the dignity of reason, the love for the nature of man all belong to man's awareness of his dignity and glory, but religion is the reminder that the glory can only be incarnate when in turning to our fellow man we take seriously the social and economic problems which he confronts and needs to resolve. Aesthetic pleasure is not the highest human achievement; the love of our fellow man in his struggle for dignity forces us to understand those "sufferings of love" which social responsibility imposes upon us. From the pure feeling for man's nature, we must come to the feeling which we should have for his suffering and needs.

This love of man is also related to our love of God. Concerning this love, Cohen makes some insightful remarks: "The love for man has therefore to be the beginning, because although God created man, man must create the fellow man for himself. And religion must assist in this creation. Thus God must become the creator of a second time when through the share of reason in religion he teaches man himself to create man as fellow man."[16] Man must indeed learn to love his fellow man before he can turn his love to God or respond to the love which God gives to him. Man must love his fellow man not merely as that other person, but so that love becomes a comprehension of the human condition, a struggle for justice and equality, an effort to grasp that dignity that lies in each being not only aesthetically as the nature of man, but concretely as a being who suffers and needs the recognition of his fellow man. The depths of Cohen's feeling of social responsibility as the source of religious commitment is shown in his clear and emphatic agreement with the prophet Isaiah, who believed that ceremony and service had little meaning unless societal responsibility moved and commanded man's actions and decisions. "The worship of God, the service, would have been to the prophets merely a spectacle, as is usual in pagan worship (tragedy originated in Dionysiac cults), if social pity had not been their basic motivation. Even the holiest day . . . is invalidated by the second Isaiah, if social pity does not govern the whole life."[17] The confrontation with the aesthetic as well as the ethical consciousness shows that only in the religious is man's distinctiveness as a being of needs and dependencies realized. From this we can comprehend the unique meaning of monotheism, a uniqueness which transcends the idea of humanity and pureness of feeling evoked by man's nature. Monotheism declares: "the poor man is your own flesh. . . . He reveals to you the fellow man. And the fellow man as the poor man brings God's love for man into the true light and the true understanding."[18] If we think of Cohen's comment about art being the particular work of art, i.e., a world for itself, *eine Welt für sich,* then we realize that the peculiarity of religion is to go beyond this individual world, to link all men to God in their poverty. Poverty is not only material, but spiritual. The uniqueness of monotheism is the universality of man's needs and dependencies before God. God's love of the stranger and the poor only points to a love which extends to all creation, to every historical reality which claims a manifestation of His love, but his love goes even beyond these, it becomes a total love, the love of all mankind. Man must learn to speak an ecumenical language to embrace this totality. Here the remarks of Cohen are decisive: "Thus he will not stop with the love for Israel only, which is merely a historical point of departure, similar to that of the stranger and the poor man. He will love man as *totality*. For he himself is not in need of man as a fellow man. For him, the correlation exists in its infinity."[19] Every historical reality is surpassed in God. The danger inherent in historical religions is the attempt to absolutize historical reality. In the *Ethics of the Pure Will,* Cohen had spoken of the unending task of the *I*. This I is not given, it is set forth as a task. "Das Individuum des reinen Willens hat seinen Brennpunkt in der unendlichen Aufgabe des Ich." The aesthetic consciousness is the feeling of the unending; here it is neither thought nor willed. When the religious is characterized as the feeling for the unending, it derives this feeling from the aesthetic. Cohen refuses to allow the religious to claim an independent feeling for the unendless. We continually want to know why he denies an independent consciousness to the religious. The answer seems to be in the fact that the religious finds its uniqueness only when and where, in relation to philosophy, it brings forth what is prepared for in philosophy, but not realized in it. Not to contradict philosophy, but to bring to it the uniqueness and incomparable value of God. We must now comprehend what this means for man as a philosophical and religious being.

Cohen denies the romantic idea that art is the source of man's dignity and worth. Art is for him only a means. Art must borrow from ethics the idea of mankind and must be inspired by it.[20] "The aesthetic consciousness alone leads to the self which finds its explanation not only in task, but which makes its task simply the individual. . . . With the concept of the individual, systematic aesthetics began: Art is the art of the genius."[21] This individuality is transfigured and transformed in the religious. God's love belongs not only to the individual, but to mankind. Mankind has a history, and it is in and through this history that we comprehend the religious feeling for the divine. Cohen affirms that we can understand history only in terms of a covenant between man and God. Man requires that his history has meaning. Neither logic, nor ethics, nor aesthetics, can give the meaning which man needs. Only religion can speak of correlation, of covenant and of Messianism. Religion creates the symbols and metaphors which allow us to grasp the sense of infinite correlation, the idealization of Israel's history, the teleological meaning of its temporal experiences. "Israel is in its history the prototype of suffering, a symbol of human suffering, of the human creature in general. God's love for Israel, no less than God's love for the poor, expresses God's love for the human race. . . . Israel is in no way an exception, but is rather the symbolic confirmation of God's love for the human race."[22] Cohen's attempt to comprehend the history of Israel is to make it meaningful not only as an individual experience, but as a human one, in and through which man can more fully grasp all the other moments of consciousness. If, for example, we attempt to comprehend the meaning of creation, we know that this idea must be embraced by the ethical, the logical, the aesthetic, and yet we know that all these moments are inadequate for the understanding of creation. Religion alone makes creation meaningful. "The creation is necessarily a continuous one, so that it means the *preservation* of the human race for the messianic realization of morality on earth. Creation, therefore, is also God's providential plan for the human race as it has already been established through God's covenant with Noah. This providential plan of world history expresses God's love for man."[23] How can we feel this love of God unless we have cultivated that aesthetic love for man's nature in all its individual expressions? The ethical idea of Humanity which we comprehend as the unending moral task is the basis of that covenant with God, in and through which we affirm trust in the future redemption of mankind. The commitment to reason, to the need for meaning, is enhanced and developed in the realization that God's revelation is deeply dependent upon the reason which is in us, which affirms its autonomy in the moral law as well as in the concept of origination, *Ursprung.*

The philosophy of history is inseparable from the meaning of man's correlation to God. History must have a judgment which is beyond itself. This judgment does not diminish history, but speaks of its purpose. What history is possible without a *telos?* Can man's search for meaning be limited to historical determinism or a relativism which reduces values to violence? Are we freed from these despairs if we discover paradigms or resign ourselves to the inadequacy of reason, to the domination of the passion, to the force of the body and the weakness of the spirit, to the cultural pessimism which denies universality and rediscovers the myths of race, nationalism, and fate? Cohen was the philosopher of optimism. The philosopher was the believer. He would have been satisfied with the remark of his former student, Ortega y Gasset: "A belief is not merely an idea that is thought, it is an idea in which one believes. And believing is not an operation of the intellectual mechanism, but a function of the living being as such, the function guiding his conduct, his performance of his task."[24] Cohen was the philosopher in whom belief and reason were in harmony. He knew that the commitment to reason was as deep and as efficacious a belief as the commitment to the moral law, to the future as the focal point of the meaning of history, and to God, before whom man recognized his dependency and his responsibility. Cohen hesitated little when he declared that "the love of God is the guiding star of world history, of whose meaning one should not despair, for it is only of today and yesterday."[25] No less fundamental than belief is hope. The philosopher who is the believer is moved by a will to the future, a hope which is rooted in a "breakthrough to universality." Here again, the words of Ortega are meaningful: "It is only under the formidable pressure of something transcendent that our person becomes compact and solid and we are enabled to discriminate between what, in effect, we are, and what we merely imagine ourselves to be."[26] The commitment of Ortega was different from that of Cohen's; yet the realization that without transcendence, neither man nor history has meaning, was the same for both. What is the purpose of all man's activities if there is no assurance that all our decisions and activities, our sufferings and beliefs, have purpose? "Monotheism is the consolation of history." From the aesthetic perspective Cohen believed that "the belief in the good is the assurance we have in the realization of the good in man's history."[27] This belief belongs to that nature of man in which the love of man has its source. Again, the aesthetic gives us the type or model; the religious, the concrete, man in relationship, standing before the "Other." The aesthetic is inadequate because it has no social dimension; it cannot be the basis for a philosophy of history. God is the source of our compassion for man. In His social love He calls forth a love which is far deeper than the sensual, a love which proceeds from the totality of our being, from "all the directions of his [man's] consciousness."

The conflict between Monotheism and the plastic arts has great meaning for Cohen's thought on the differences between aesthetics and religion. In the Aesthetic, Cohen says of the plastic arts: "The unity which was created between body and soul in the form of man can now cover the unity between man and God. As the Greek spirit was led by the principle of identity, 'Everything is divine and the human is everything,' so no object can be given between heaven and earth which can and must not be drawn into the realm of the plastic arts. The gods were formed as if they were men, and men were elevated to the ideal form of the gods. Life is not only the struggle of men and peoples, but also the gods struggle with and for men and people."[28] Having given this evaluation of the relationship between gods and men, Cohen in his religion of reason declares that for the monotheistic religious consciousness there must be a refusal of the plastic arts. Nothing was more objectionable to Cohen than the pantheism which he believed motivated Spinoza and his followers, Schelling and Hegel. "Nowhere do we recognize so clearly that compelling inner consequence of fundamental ideas as the dependence of philosophical romanticism upon Spinoza. Schelling and Hegel . . . are both captured by pantheism. The danger of pantheism does not lie originally in the threat to the God idea. This is its consequence. The error of the pantheistic principle and fundament lies in the concept of man and the problem of ethics. If God and nature are the same, then man and nature are at least the same. Therefore, the difference between Being and the Should Be is eliminated."[29] The consequence of this identification is clear: Ethics is dissolved into Logic, man's freedom to decide, to act, and to realize the self as task does not exist. The identity-philosophy of German idealism reduces God to a logical category and thus eliminates Him. This idealism reduces philosophy to theogony and human life to the demonic intercourse with divinity.

The plastic arts were rejected by the prophets, lyric poetry became the vehicle of monotheism. "Is this a contradiction against the unity of the arts in the unity of the aesthetic consciousness? There is no contradiction."[30] Human consciousness does not belong exclusively to the aesthetic. Religion has its own reality of God in correlation to man, and if it doesn't find the plastic arts to be receptive to this correlation, because of the consequences of the identity embraced in them, then it turns to lyric poetry for what it could not find in the plastic arts. Lyric poetry is an expression of man's longing, *Sehnsucht,* for God, but this longing is rooted in man's compassion for his fellow man. Cohen continuously ties every mode of relationship between God and man to one between man and man. "Compassion toward man is the other side of the longing for God."[31] No clearer statement can be given as a guide for Cohen's religious philosophy. Religion, revealed in its intimate tie between God and man, is philosophical in its belief that the man-to-man relationship is at its core and is thus the base from which it develops. Whatever we say about Cohen, this relationship remains fundamental. The poets of the Psalms are the creators of religion, their poetry is the fundamental element of pure feeling, in them monologue becomes dialogue. Dialogue separates radically indentity-philosophy from monotheism. In the Aesthetics, Cohen clarifies this difference, Poetry becomes the dialogue of the Psalms: "Longing is the most inward intensification simply through the idealization of the self. Nevertheless, this idealization can never destroy the multiplicity and ambiguity which are linked to the I. . . . The monologue of longing becomes dialogue, a duel of lovers or of a partner in different stages of his love, or with the multiple cooperation of other affects."[32] If, indeed, in the plastic arts the purity of monotheism is endangered, then this danger is reflected in the lack of truthfulness which accompanies every identification of God with the human form. Cohen speaks of the shame which is incurred in idolatry. Truthfulness is the deepest embrace of the Psalms. The truth of God is that He is like no man. His truth is this radical separation. The truthfulness of man is the acknowledgment of this truth. Every philosophy that stands in truth must begin with this recognition. "If He were man He could not be the God of truth, and, hence, man can only become truthful through the truth of his God, who is not man."[33] Monotheism is opposed to the plastic arts. It is endangered by every philosophical system which is analogous to this art. It is threatened by totality and the monologue which it embodies. When the real and reasonable become one, then Being and the Should Be are identical. Here logic and ethics are not only unified, but logic absorbs ethics. Schelling and Hegel are the philosophers of the plastic arts.

"Truth establishes truthfulness, and truthfulness is the backbone of the moral man. Thanks to the power of religious truthfulness, the moral man is the religious man. And the religious man is the historical man."[34] The strength of Cohen's philosophy of religion is the truth upon which it is based, and the truthfulness which it requires of man. The truth of God's uniqueness is the source of Cohen's belief, and the cause of his rejection of every philosophical system which violates the separation of man and God. Pantheism had to be overcome if philosophy was to rest upon a truth which allowed it to be truthful. This meant for Cohen the autonomy of reason, the moral law, and the love of man's nature. Compassion toward our fellow man is the source of our love of God. The goodness of man's nature is realized in compassion; man's longing for the good in the recognition of God as truth. The philosopher cannot but be the believer, for in truth philosophy has its beginning; its end is the realization of this truth. The dialogue which it realizes is that of reason, the universal dialogue of reason, the dialogue of truthfulness. The same dialogue reflects upon the question of the plastic arts and asks if the "monotheistic concept of man could have originated at all if it had been formed in close connection with the development of the concept of God in the plastic arts."[35] The problem forces us to rethink the history of philosophy and the concept of man. Cohen was certain that monotheism required an independence from the concepts of man and God formed in the plastic arts and the pantheistic philosophies which continually develop from them. Cohen raised the further question of whether "the peculiar kind of poetry of the Bible could have arisen if the plastic arts had not been checked. This peculiarity consists in the lyric poetry of the Psalms, which sing neither of God alone nor of man alone."[36] The problems which Cohen raises in these remarks reveal moral, ethical, and aesthetic implications which force us to reconsider the nature of philosophy and its history. The consequences are serious for those who are committed to reason, and who believe that dialogue, the universal discourse of reason, is inseparable from God's correlation with man.

9

Hermann Cohen and W. A. Mozart

Music, art, and poetry were profound forces in Hermann Cohen's thought. If we attempt to comprehend this philosopher, whose name is synonymous with the School of Marburg, that small charming town in Hanover from where Kant's works and influence spread abroad like the magic of an irresistible melody, then we are forced to appreciate those lovers of music and art that brought him the friendship of the violinist Joseph Joachim, the admiration of painters such as Max Liebermann, Lenid Pasternak (the father of Boris), and others whose names are now distant from us.[1] European culture is alive in philosophy not merely as illustrative references, but as the achievements of the mind devoted to reason and power of imagination. This culture was not simply created by a mind that ignored the senses. The body was appreciated as the source of subtle and artistic movement, its power to build and form depended upon the grace and delicacy of the hands. Sound awakened in us the inexhaustible dimension and possibilities of communication and relationship, sight the sensitivity to colors, to a variety of architectural forms that evoke a sense of beauty and sublimity by their effect and receptivity. Taste and touch cultivate form and allow us to receive and be receptive with a heightened sense of delicacy and appreciation allowing form to be given to us in indescribable and unexpected ways. Through the senses we develop that intimacy with our fellow man that the mind can only define and analyze, but never feels. Cohen has come forth from his detractors and even from his admirers as the distant and unapproachable "professor" of a forgotten philosophical "system." He did his service in Kant's army of interpreters adding volumes of interpretation and appreciation to the old master. Here he paid his dues to his profession and university. Cohen was a cultured man, a deeply sensitive individual, a fine product of artistic sensitivity and generosity. When he turned to the arts, when he moved to music, to religion, to social activity, the humaneness of his personality overcame the professor in him; it showed that tenderness for human relationship, that deep love that Cohen found in Wolfgang Amadeus Mozart, whose operas he believed reflected a sensitivity to moral and aesthetic values.

At the end of his article on "Mozart's Opera Texts," written in honor of Mozart's 150th birthday, Cohen called him the world citizen of a coming humanity, the *Weltbuerger einer kommenden Menschheit*.[2] This encomium expressed the purpose and meaning of the philosophical endeavor. What is this love of wisdom that philosophers have so easily spoken of if not the persistent venture to comprehend human nature, to discover those ties that link man to nature and nature to man. Man is bound to man when he grasps how he belongs to nature and what is nature in him. Through the intellect man strives to conquer nature, to subordinate it to the logic of his reason, to make it a tool of his activity, the glory of his intellectual ambition. Reading Cohen's *Logic of Pure Knowledge* forces us to conclude that he believed this to be the truth. With all the power of his intellect he unfolded for us an Idealism in which the sublimity of the mind showed its uniqueness in such a way that its power of transformation and transfiguration swept before it the senses and whatever content failed to yield to this conquering reason. Could we expect of this philosopher in whom Hellenism and Hebraism launched its most challenging attack on nature with the slogan: "The Conquest of Nature," to be receptive, sensitive, and profoundly open to the moments of life where passion is man's fundamental drive? Could we imagine the philosopher of the pure will, a reality conjured in the philosopher's mind, but nowhere alive in human relationships to be immersed in understanding the differences between the passions of Figaro and Don Giovanni?[3] There is in Cohen this multiplicity of perspectives and involvements that defy facile summaries of his thought. They are only possible with the help of ignorance.

"The Magic Flute," Mozart's last opera, was the object of Cohen's deepest musical love. Karl Löwith points to Cohen's lifelong devotion to the great works of world literature. From the Mozart text he drew "the brotherhood of man, the peace of God's kingdom on earth." He spoke of the "Messianism of the Magic Flute."[4] We could refer to these designations as intellectual jargon if we had refused to read the libretto and attempt to comprehend Cohen's immersion in it as a mere desire to be sensitive to human life and its aspirations in its passionate and indefinable possibilities. Human life is an infinite series of adventure and dreams, foolishnesses and tragedies, pains and joys. Here meanings are multiple and so diverse that only a fool would dare attempt to bring them within concepts and ideas. Perhaps the supreme danger lies in the absence of imaginative adventure, dreams and humor. Despair or pessimism, surrender or fatalism denies comedy and tragedy, it refuses humor and deadens life. There was, indeed, meaning for Cohen, perhaps not only in dream and adventure, but in that sense of humanity that we develop in feeling and in sensitivity, in intimate contact with life. Cohen was always more than epistemologist.

Löwith points out how much Cohen loved those magnificent duets between Papagena and Pagageno and between Pagageno and Pamina. Our concern is to find out what in these duets was so meaningful to Cohen. Cohen had at the beginning of his analysis of "The Magic Flute" stated in abstract terms what it meant to him: "the moral Ideal, the brotherhood of man, peace on earth, and in the reality of politics, in the life of man and nations."[5] The outline of the story of "The Magic Flute" is easily understood. A prince, Pamino, is tempted by a picture to go in search of a beautiful princess, the daughter of the Queen of the Night. He is accompanied by Papageno, a bird catcher, who is in search of a wife. They come to the temple of Isis and Osiris, meet the High Priest Sarastro and discover the teachings of this temple to be the purest expression of the Ideal of love and humaneness. What is of overwhelming beauty are the melodic duets and the feelings they evoke and express. Papageno's dream is to find the pretty girl "to love and cherish tenderly. I'd bring her cake and sugarplums, and be content to eat the crumbs. She'd share my little nest with me; a happier pair could never be."[6] Papageno is an ordinary man, he does not need to live with ideas, ideals, logic or in fact he does not need to think. When, after meeting Tamino, he is asked by him, "But by what do you live?" Papageno replies, "by eating and drinking, just as everyone else does."[7] Fundamentally in eating and drinking all men find a unity and a need to satisfy wants, and a responsibility to contribute to this satisfaction. Cohen, we should remark, was a socialist in Kantian guise. Men are never means but ends. Law and society exist for the realization of human equality, to ameliorate suffering and give educational possibilities to all who must develop their reason. Human suffering and pain were concrete societal responsibilities. No moral man can ignore the sufferings of his fellow-men.

Tamino tries to explain the power that love has in him. "O image, angel-like and fair! No mortal can with thee compare! I feel it, how this godly sight pervades my heart with new delight. I cannot name the strange desire which burns my heart with glowing fire. Can this emotion love reveal?"[8] The music, the voice, the incomparable beauty of Mozart's melodic genius give these words their overwhelming affect that communes with us in such a way that subjects and objects are dissolved in sound and a peculiar and unique unity is achieved. Here we discover what it is to be beyond subject and object, to remain in the non-defensible and non-determinable, to feel the dissolution of those forms so dear to logic, to discover reality without limits and forms that transcend form. Form and content find their own inexpressible joining and immersion in an endless evolutionary interaction.

To ease his way, Tamino is given the magic flute. "More gold than gold and treasure a magic flute like this is worth; by its spell would human woe change to happiness and mirth."[9] We think of love as delicate and beautiful and we are correct, but love is painful suffering, and forever at work. Cohen was deeply attached to the love duet, its sadness and joy, its hope and despair; Cohen had developed duets with every aspect of human creativity. In the particular duet between Papageno and Pamena, Papageno tells her that Tamino loves her and she replies: "Love? He loves me, then? Oh, say that again! It feels so good to hear the world 'love'!" Papageno feels deeply his own need to love, to find a Papagena. "Sometimes I feel like ripping out all my feathers when I see that Papageno has not found a Papagena yet," Pamina replies sadly. She knows that each man must have a wife and each woman a husband. "Have patience, friend. The Gods will take care of you. They will send you a wife, before you even think." Papageno only wishes that the Gods would act quickly and both sing: "Let joyous love for grief atone, we live by love, by love alone." Pamina continues: "To love's sweet might yields every creature. It offers everlasting joy." The last lines of the duet are: "Its noble aim shows clear in life; no greater good than man and wife. Wife and man, and man and wife, reach the height of godly life."[10] The duet needs little comment. It is a sensitive expression of human needs, the joy that comes with sharing, devotion and responsibility. Cohen was deeply affected by this power of love and we wonder why something so human and necessary arouses such strong interest in such a man. Cohen is a great thinker because it does.

Tamino is told to be "silent, steadfast and forbearing." The words have a peculiar power. Cohen believed that Germany would be the true home of the Jew. Love would unite one people with the other; it demanded steadfastness, courage, and above all, patience. Cohen loved his homeland. He was a deep believer in its greatness. He hoped that it would love him. Could he imagine that it would exterminate his wife in 1942, in Theresienstadt?[11] Love was for Cohen as vital as it was fleeting and beyond reach. He reached out to Mozart like a brother in whom is found that love that he knew was the passion that gave and took life. Cohen was firmly aware of the cultural despair, pessimism, sexual perversities, myths and aphoristic attempts at philosophy that controlled his age. The peoples he loved, the great literature he adored, the art and music he found in Rembrandt and Mozart were peaks and rareties, easily consumed by the ignorance and mythical prejudices he found around him. He loved a homeland and a God. He loved a contradiction.

Tamino's love was Pamina. The spirits tell him: "Have courage, prince, brave be and proud. Then you will win by manly daring. Ponder: *Kurz, sei ein Mann.*"[12] There is an optimism in Mozart that deeply touched Cohen. Courage and strength will conquer. With these manly virtues we storm the gates of ignorance and myth, put aside the wild furies of the ego; we will restore a sense of responsibility and the dignity of reason. We give man again that hard but valued task of "daring to know," the search for universality, preserving the right to think of the Ideal, of Humanity. Before the unknown temple Tamino says: "Where man is achieving and idleness banned. There vice and dishonesty never may stand. I enter the gate and all peril defy! My purpose is blameless and noble and high."[13] Tamino, who had not known if Pamina was alive, discovers that she lives and what had occurred since her abduction and her escape from Monostatos, the Moor, who wanted to make her his wife. With Papageno, Pamina is safe. He has fended off Monostatos with his magic bells and both sing: "If to every honest man bells like these were given, all his foes would swiftly then far away be driven. He would live contentedly, in the sweetest harmony. Only friendship's harmony lessens pain and grieving. Without friendly sympathy, joy this earth is leaving."[14] Mozart's music is Cohen's pure will, the pure response of man to the divinity of reason that he knows to be in him and for which he has assumed responsibility and which is the source of his hope and faith. With this music creation is redeemed and man transfigured.

Sarastro, the High Priest, bade Tamino, Papageno and Pamina to enter the temple. "To enter our temple, these strangers may not be denied. So let their heads be covered then; they must at first be purified."[15] Tamino will become a member of the temple, but he first must face the ordeals that await him. Sarastro orders Papageno and Tamino to be brought before him. "Let Tamino and his companion be led into the court of the temple (to the speaker, who kneels before him) and you, friend, fulfill your holy office and teach to both what duty to humanity is; teach them to perceive the might of the gods."[16] What is the might of these gods? Reward for virtue and punishment for vice. Tamino shall be dedicated to this morality: *der Tugend Lohn, dem Laster aber Strafe seien.* This morality seems indeed to be noble and grand. Cohen says that the text of "The Magic Flute" is a religiosity that is without being a book religion, *die hoechste Religiositaet ohne Buchreligion.*"[17] There is more to be said. These beautiful, and, perhaps, sublime words and thoughts, rarely touch more than a few rare beings. Papageno has something else to say about this struggle Tamino is undertaking and about the noble simplicity it proclaims. "Fighting is not exactly in my line. To be truthful, I don't demand any wisdom, either. I'm just a child of nature, who is satisfied with sleep, food, and drink. And if I once could catch a pretty little wife...."[18] This "child of nature" who speaks of sleep, food and drink, knows also of love, the need to share, to have something pretty and to know responsibility and virtue. In Papageno's song men find that clear and precise reality that is the foundation of all thinking: with needs begins thinking. Needs unite us in universality with mankind, they deepen and develop our feeling for man. Oblivious to needs, how is it possible to speak of feeling, to comprehend the will as demand, to understand that love creates and the stranger becomes a fellow being? In it lies universal religiosity.

Monostatos, the Moor, appears and bewails his fate. "All the world is full of lovers, man and maiden, bud and bee. Why am I not like the others? No one ever looks at me! Why should I not be a match for some delightful demoiselle? If I were to die a bachelor, I prefer to live in hell!"[19] Monostatos who would like to kiss Pamina seems to reflect that universal cry of the black men that his feelings are not the same as that of other men. *Weil ein Schwarzer haesslich ist!*" Monostatos is barbarous in the expression of his passion, but there are in him feelings that link him to all men. Below the artificiality of race there is communality. Cohen knew the vile levels of anti-Semitism and their destructive characterizations. He knew them from his students. Were not his lectures on Schiller ridiculed? Should the Jew call Schiller "our Schiller"? In spite of this we msut believe that there is a growing consciousness on all levels of existence, that there is a widening spiritual dimension, that man is evolving consciously in a universe that is growing, that there is an expanding spiritual realm that infuses all others and will one day make more and more men aware that in us there is a growing consciousness forming a community of mankind.

It is poor Papageno who finds his trials difficult. Tamino has already become a devoted believer. He says to Sarastro: "My faithful heart is yours alone. *Wird ewig Dein Getreuer sein.*"[20] Papageno, however, sings his disdain. "I don't care a fig about the ordained. Anyway, there are more people like me in the world. At the moment, to me the greatest pleasure would be a glass of wine.... With no one to love me or care I'll certainly die of despair. I'd give my finest feather, etc. ... With no one to give me affection I'm buried in hopeless dejection! But all that I need is a kiss to put me in heavenly bliss."[21] Papageno speaks of the bliss that is within his grasp. What more does he need to satisfy his existence than drink, sleep and a woman. Papageno is free of doubt, he knows the fickleness of life, its needs and satisfaction. There is truth in Papageno's remark. Life can be satisfied without thinking. The passions are deeper in their needs than thinking. The violence that is at the source of life evokes reason that reflects on it and calls it negation. Reason can be inadequate to the negation that it creates. Papageno would rather have the old, ugly woman than no woman at all. His Papagena was disguised as an old woman. "Renounce the world forever? Drink water? No! In that case I'll take an old one rather than none at all. Well, here you have my hand with the assurance that I shall always be true to you (aside) until I find someone prettier,"[22] Papageno sings. We do not become thinkers unless we satisfy needs. Philosophy begins with the need to speculate, to comprehend the meaning of our relationship with nature, with our senses and their reality, with what we call receptivity and autonomy.

Tamino is pledged to silence. Pamina does not understand his obligation to Sarastro and feels that he no longer loves her. The "boys" tell her to control her grief. "This to tell thee is forbidden, but no longer be it hidden that his heart is thine alone. He is faithful, he is wise, even death for thee defies. Come, Tamino waits for thee!" Pamina is now assured and sings: "Two hearts which love has bound together, the storms of life will firmly weather. No foe will threaten them with wrath. The Gods will smile upon their path."[23] Love is the sacred power that creates the links that bind man to woman and woman to man. Love is that magic power that gives faith to the idea of Humanity and to which man's most precious creations owe their allegiance. Has love still to become love? We should speak of the evolutionary force of love. We think of God as the endless fulfillment of an evolving consciousness. The Idea of Humanity is in its infancy, the world is only slowly becoming conscious of its endless potential for relationship and growth. Cohen's messianic hopes lay in his awareness that the spirit had only just begun to comprehend its potentiality and possibility.

The end of the opera brings with it that tender and affectionate duet between Papageno and Papagena. Papageno had not yet found his Papagena when he sang: "Sick and tired am I of living. Since my love was all in vain, I shall die to end my pain. Yonder tree shall be my gallows." The little boys console him and tell him to ring his magic bells and his Papagena will appear. She does and the two sing: "What a joy for us is near when the gods, their bounty showing, and their grace on us bestowing will send us tiny children dear. First we will have a Papageno, then we will have a Papagena"[24] and then more Papagenos and Papagenas. They sing the joy of love and child. Cohen was deeply touched with this duet. He was sensitive to love and human relationship, to pain and happiness. He deeply understood the vital necessity of family life, faithfulness, trust, courage and endurance. Moral life he knew was the preparation for moral philosophy. Moral life made the philosopher a companion for his fellowman. His existence and thought must favor and augment the quality of life about and beyond him. Cohen comprehended philosophy in a deeply human sense, he felt the need to take responsibility for the needs of his fellow-men. There was in him a faithfulness to the demand which the feeling for man placed upon him. This tender and yet profound duet he loved because it so deeply sang the most deep-felt longings of man and woman, that search for happiness in mutual love.

The final words of the opera are those of the chorus preceded by those of the High Priest Sarastro. "The sun's radiant glory has vanquished the night. The powers of darkness have yielded to the light." The chorus sings: "Hail to thee, great Isis! Hail to thee, Osiris! You guided their ways. Praise, praise, praise to thee, Osiris. Thanks, thanks to Isis we raise! Thus courage has triumphed and virtue will rise, the laurels of wisdom receiving as prize."[25] It is to wisdom that we give honor and hope to receive from her the reward that comes with virtue and courage. What more do we ask from our ventures in this world, our struggle with racism and atavistic ignorance. We hear the opera, we see its actions, we witness man's folly and strength, his joy and pain, his dreams and hopes. We struggle for meaning and grasp its terrifying demands. It is too much for us and yet we dare not hide in simplistic formulae and clever logical games. We differentiate between illusions and fact but we know that both are essential to our earthly ventures. The only evil is resignation, that cultural despair and pessimism that Cohen deeply feared. Nothing must turn us from the value of life, the struggle for knowledge, the demand of the pure will, the sublimity of the pure feeling in which we find that immediacy with man's creative expressions in literature, art, music and in the limitless expansion of knowledge and moral consciousness. Cohen loved the opera because it was a love duet, the brotherhood of man sings its wonders and hears the pain and folly of life, hears the cues of the passions and knows they are truths, hears the sadness and the joys, the ideals and momentary actions, joins in humor what is comical and tragic and forces us to surpass every moment that encompasses it and claims exclusivity. Humor surpasses every moment and quality of life. Cohen comprehended it with depth and meaning.

Having analyzed the text of the opera we must now ask about its significance in Cohen's philosophy, in particular his *Aesthetics*. We must then inquire about the relationship between the *Aesthetics* and Cohen's philosophy of religion, in particular, *Der Begriff der Religion im System der Philosophie* (*The Concept of Religion in the System of*

Philosophy). From these considerations we could draw some conclusions about aesthetics, religion and the Idea of Humanity. The concluding sentences of Cohen's article on Mozart are revealing. "Freemasonry was his [Mozart's] political love. He believed in it completely. The brotherhood of man was his belief and longing. The mystery of this secret organization was his politics. This man of the 18th century, the age of the Emperor Joseph, was a great artist of the German spirit (Geist). As a German citizen he was a world citizen of a coming humanity."[26] Much of what Cohen says of Mozart he would say of himself. Although not a freemason, Cohen linked the German spirit to the coming age of humanity. He saw himself as the inheritor of this Mozart *Geist*. Cohen had his own "Beloved Community" of universal spirits from Plato to Kant. All belonged to the Temple whose allegiance was to love and whose Idea was universality and community. He liked so speak of the humanity of an artist. He spoke of *die Humanitaet Homers;* Cohen's ultimate loyalty was to this universal community of men whose idea was similar to his. Cohen's expression of it was also deeply practical. The problems of the day were his concerns. He was political in activity and thought. He lived with the idea that man must never be a means for any government or system of thought; he was always an end.

The "Preface" to his *Aesthetics of the Pure Will* is a clear statement of what aesthetics means to Cohen. "The purpose of my book is to defend the inherent right of world historical philosophy. What would philosophy be if only the art historian or the artist had the right to philosophize about art?"[27] Every aspect of human creativity belongs to philosophical investigation. In philosophy all these activities have their origin. Philosophy teaches systematic thinking; it enables us to create those categories that make coherent discourse a possibility. Philosophy is a challenge to the how and the why of our thinking. The philosopher knows that he belongs to a community of interpretation that allows him to become more deeply aware of the nature of his thought and to the negation that is embodied within it. "The classical symbol of art is eternity. Through the centuries this eternity remains alive in the sensitive observer. He belongs to the reality, is part of its proof, he belongs to the highest moment of the world history of art."[28] Cohen now remarks that he who "philosophizes about art must seek to fill his heart with the world of art, like the man who thinks of nature, since a universe must be a problem. Man philosophizes about a world soul when he thinks of the world of art. The universe of art must be present to the inner life of the man who wants to be prepared for aesthetics." This capacity to fill the soul with the great works of art means to develop that sensitivity to human creativity, to be conscious of form as beauty, to cultivate the imagination with symbols and metaphors, to grasp that architecture of the mind that lies open to the unexpected and unknown as the sources of artistic and aesthetic experience. The tenderness which we have for variety and change, must accompany a capacity for contradiction, ugliness and contradiction. The beautiful is joined with the painful, wisdom with folly, the clear with the obtuse. When Cohen speaks of the heart filled with a world of art, he speaks of that education of the feeling that makes possible our capacity to comprehend life in all its multiplicity and manifoldness. We can understand that only pessimism and despair, resignation and hopelessness destroy that openness to aesthetic pleasure and that feeling for all things human.

Cohen wanted to make two things clear in his aesthetics: "1) the distinction between the aesthetics of art history and the science and development of the arts. 2) the definition of philosophical aesthetics as systematic, as a discipline that belongs to the system of philosophy and has its methodological center in this system."[30] Aesthetics, like ethics and a theory of knowledge, is a fundamental expression of its spirit. It is as absolute in its purity and as free from external condition as the other systematic constituents. Pure feeling is evoked from the beauty and sublimity of creation, from humanity in human relationship, from the love that drives man and woman to each other. We need only recall these duets that Cohen so deeply loved. Cohen's attraction for the masterpieces of literature, art, and music was rooted in that feeling they caused in him, that intimate, tender and sensitive attachment they created between him and mankind. To teach this pure feeling was a goal of his philosophical activity. He calls art a *Herzkeraft*. Cohen envisioned philosophy as *Kulturphilosophie* in which the particular expressions were, in the broadest sense, Logic, Ethics, and Aesthetics. Philosophy "stands on these three feet. Philosophy is not something above and beyond them."[31]

Culture embraces man's coherent discourse. Man discourses about ethics, aesthetics, logic; each discourse is inseparable from the other. What is knowledge that is not loved or felt to be beautiful? What is more sublime than the categorical imperative? What arouses feelings more deeply than human suffering and joy, form, and that amazing discovery of the mind's architecture, measure? What fascinates us more thoroughly than the workings of the human body? The dance, the forming power of the hands, their capacity to do wonders through their physical structure. The structure of bodily form, of natural form are the wonders that excite our imagination, drive us to know and force us to do with trust and love what enhances the feeling for humanity in us.

Cohen continues his analysis of *Kulturphilosophie*. "Systematic philosophy has its root in the thought that all problems of culture arise from the common source of reason in its unity and maturity and not from individual means, suggestions and disclosures of consciousness for which the spirit (*Geist*) cannot be responsible."[32] Then he repeats a thought that has always been fundamental. "We must slowly realize that only the scientific (*wissenschaftliche*) reason is the criterion of human reason, only the scientific spirit establishes the worth of the human spirit. Rationalism develops into Idealism, to methodic, mature, scientific Rationalism."[33] Reason that is constantly comprehending itself as reason and method that is persistently attempting to ground method in method is worthy of being method. Method is neither fixed nor absolute. It is critique always being subject to critique. Cohen's strong belief that the scientific spirit is the criterion of human reason is important if we understand that thinking is always thinking about the procedures of thinking; thinking is the formation of the categories in and through which thinking attempts to structure a discourse about the subject and object of reason. Idealism or rationalism is the refusal to allow thought to be anything else than critique, the realization that whatever is must find the means to be expressed and created as thought. What refuses to be embodied in thought has no meaning for it. Thought is not simply a theory of knowledge; it is also will and feeling, but in thought they can be spoken of as *pure* will and *pure* feeling. As *pure* they reveal Reason as source of everything that man would bring forth if he were to actualize the spirit in him. Reason as source is man's future reality. In each moment of time the philosopher who is committed to Reason attempts to comprehend it. This struggle for comprehension within Reason is Cohen's Idealism. Idealism is reason comprehending itself as Reason.

Cohen was convinced that art is a vital measure of a culture. "For all questions of contemporary culture, art is in the center. Here the problem of Idealism is fought."[34] The cultivation of taste is not simply linked to the gratification of the senses, it requires the development of the judgment, of that universality of communication that enhances interest in the beautiful, in the pleasure that arises in form. This pleasure does not come forth only from the fine arts but belongs to the form, moral responsibility and action.

Communicability that enhances community, that enlivens our sensitivities and struggle for meaning and coherence is an object of beauty. Every society struggles to enhance its universality of thought, the quality of its concern for the particular social, moral and political needs. The tastes that it instils in its youth is the measure of its cultural awareness. Taste measures the degree of civilization a society has achieved. Cohen was one of the last European philosophers with Husserl, Cassirer, and Löwith, who believed that European civilization was its master thinkers: Homer, Virgil, Dante, Shakespeare, Leonardo da Vinci, Goethe, Valéry, and its artists, scientists and philosophers. Philosophy was for him the engagement in all the forms of human creativity. He was a lover of the idea of humanity. He could say, without embarrassment, that he loved ideas. He refused every attitude that deprived him of his responsibility to philosophy as the *Kulturphilosophie*.

Kant wrote in his *Anthropology* that "the one universal characteristic of madness is loss of *common sense* (sensus *communis*) and the substitution of logical private sense *(sensus privatus)* for it."[35] Kant believed that a common sense was the basis for the judgment of taste. "Only under the presupposition, I repeat, of such a common sense, are we able to lay down a judgment of taste."[36] The common sense is the presupposition for universal communicability and community. The education of the common sense in reason is the end of every enlightened society. For Cohen the common sense was the "great community" of reason.

The exclusivity of the private sense deprives us of that communion and communicability that forms and advances the idea of that "community of interpretation" which we have called the universe of coherent discourses. Kant wrote that "we have to attach our own understanding to the *understanding of other* men too, instead of *isolating* ourselves with our own understanding and still wishing our private ideas to judge publicly, so to speak."[37] Assuming that we are speaking as reasonable men we suppose that we need the understanding of other men. Unless we have reduced our language to commands or revelations we know that the need to convince depends upon judgment and reasonableness. Common sense allows us to assume reasonableness, the private sense facilitates our return to myth and dream. "A man who pays not attention to this criterion but obstinately recognizes private sense as already valid apart from or even in opposition to common sense is abandoned to a play of thought in which he sees, conducts and judges himself, not in a world in common with others, but in his own world (as in dreaming)."[38] Cohen knew even more deeply the consequences of the *sensus privatus,* the cultural despair and pessimism it drew from itself, the myth and dreams it conjured from its condemnation and hatred of society, from the fatalism of the historical schemes it created to justify its refusal to take responsibility to build a world in common with others. Cohen feared deeply the atavism and nationalism that destroy the belief in the idea of Humanity. He knew what disastrous consequences reasonable men suffer in a society whose common sense was nothing more than the fantasies of the private sense.

In Cohen's definition of Ideals we find the guide to all aspects of his thought:

> Idealism is the word in which the German spirit joins the original power, *Urkraft,* of Greece.... This fundamental word should not be reduced to a slogan for nationalist blindness and for a false, narrow, self-seeking patriotism, even less should it become an enticing term for a philosophy that impugns the sovereignty of rationalism. It must be protected from thoughtless misuse and, above all, frivolity. It must be a holy exhortation to the unceasing justification of culture before the forum of scientific reason.[39]

Idealism is the freedom of the spirit that transcends borders and peoples, that takes its abode wherever and whenever man is conscious of himself as the discoverer of reason. Spirit knows neither national type nor land as its specific and unique soil. Cohen's belief in Idealism was his commitment to the spirit as rational critique. This critique is understood when it is expressed negatively as the distinct refusal to identify thinking with myth, aphoristic language and above all, the attempt to reduce philosophy to ontology, to identify time with presence and thus transfigure it into fate and necessity. Cohen returned to the past, struggled in the present, but above all, fought for the future. From the weight of future responsibility and demand the religious and moral world discovered hope, trust, and responsibility. Philosophy was for Cohen a matter of trust. Idealism arises from the freedom to trust, to know that what we discover to be the spirit is the ground of logic, the responsibility of moral command, and that feeling which responds to the Idea of community and power of love. In Idealism we discover the Cohen who loved "The Marriage of Figaro," "Don Giovanni," "The Magic Flute," who sang the love duets, who was sensitive to passion and who revered reason and wisdom. The evolution of divinity is necessitated by that human evolution in which man is forever discovering, that never-ending consciousness that penetrates, if but slowly, what we call reality. Here we glimpse that universality that binds humanity to divinity.

In his final remarks, Cohen wrote of his hopes for the *Aesthetics*. "The highest, *das Hoechste,* that I can wish for this book is that it may help make possible the honesty and respectability in the use of the magnificent word, Idealism, that it enjoyed in classical philosophy since Plato, and bring back again man's feeling for the word."[40] Cohen was willing to link religion closely to Idealism and ask: "Can religion today purify itself through pure morality without Idealism? Can it, in turning away from this purification, achieve its historical development?" Turning to politics, Cohen asked: "As paradoxical as it may seem today is not Idealism for politics the most reliable guide? All in all, it is the final and only help."[41] These questions and these hopes belong to the architecture of Cohen's thought and activity. The belief in the Idea and in the future, in Humanity and in the God of moral demand are Cohen's philosophical beliefs. They are the beliefs of his reason. He was steeped in the nobility and truthfulness of the Idea and the responsibility it placed upon the man who could hear its command, see in its light, comprehend the power it had upon reality and the formative force it brought about for those who formed community in devotion to its validity. Religion is myth and demonic subjection to past historical events without the purity of the ethical will, without that love that calls forth divinity as the Love of love. The love of God belongs not only to the present but to the future. We must be aware that mankind's capacity for this love is only beginning. This seems paradoxical, to the same degree, as the political seems in relationship to Idealism, as nascent and limited. It makes no sense to speak of the Idea of God unless we have made room for belief through our love for the transcendent. It makes little sense to speak of a *Rechtsstaat* unless we face the rights and needs of the power state and *Staatsraison* with courage and hope. The philosopher is the guardian of culture. He must and should hold forth to his fellow-man not only what *is,* but what *should be.* Cohen once observed that the truthfulness of the German spirit would be determined by the choice it makes between Kant or Hegel, *ob Kant oder Hegel.* "German Idealism is Kant's Idealism."[42] In this Idealism there is universal community.

Cohen then made a sharp distinction between Idealism and philosophical pretext or *Scheinphilosophie.* "What we call in antiquity, sophism, is nothing more than philosophical pretext, which, in contrast to scientific Idealism, wants to reveal the sense of the world. The sense of the world is, however, peculiarly and uniquely the spirit (*der Geist*) of philosophy bound to science (*Wissenschaft*)."[43] This clear and precise attempt to set forth the goal of his thought bears in it Cohen's undeniable belief in radical monotheism. Kant had stated that "there is no more sublime passage in the Jewish Law than the commandment, Thou shall not make unto thee any graven image, or any likeness of any thing that is in heaven or on earth or under the earth."[44] For Cohen, the graven images of immediate existence and its categories were only the realities of a moment that pretends to be absolute. These were in tension with the world of Ideas that lend their facticity, a temporary and arbitrary quality. What stood over and opposed to given existence was a reality that was *yet to be,* that would transform and transfigure the world it opposed as its contrary. This was not a substitution of one existence for another, but the appearance of the Idea and the Ideal as moral command. What, however, is command to man for whom there is only the moment and unmediated reality? Like the power of love, the future depends upon our capacity for its receptivity. Moral life is preparation for moral universality. The religion of reason is prepared in the comprehension of the nature of moral and aesthetic activity. Where societal existence has made no preparation for taste and responsibility, ethics and aesthetics remain tools of the philosophers. We can experience only what we are receptive to and this depends upon education and the satisfaction of needs. Papageno wanted drink, sleep and food. He needed a woman to love. The satisfaction of man's wants is the preparation for taste and morality. Cohen knew this well. He was a philosopher but also a fellowman. He knew the power of feelings.

Three years after Cohen left Marburg, in 1912, he published *The Concept of Religion in the System of Philosophy*. The chapter concerning the relationship between aesthetics and religion concerns our discussion. Cohen distinguished between aesthetic love as *eros* and the religious love for man. "The aesthetic love is *eros,* it is pure creative feeling bringing forth a work of art and verifying itself in this creation. This creative feeling of love for man's nature is not the religious love of man. Religion cannot think the individual, but its specific vehicle, love, grasps him in this peculiar particularity which is transformed into individuality."[45] It seems that Cohen who neither discovered individuality in logic nor in ethics and aesthetics then found in religious love that intimate and unique relationship in which individuality is the primal element. The individuality that Cohen stressed was not a privacy between God and man, but one rooted in man's suffering. *"Die religioese Liebe entzuendet sich am Leiden des Menschen.''*[46] Man's suffering unites man to man and man to God. Art, Cohen asserted, speaks of the ugly, *die Haesslichkeit.* Ugliness and sublimity belong to the beautiful. Cohen cited the final scene of Plato's *Symposium* in which Alcibiades speaks of Socrates. Cohen highlighted the comparison that Alcibiades made between Socrates and Silenus, and again with Marsyas the Satyr:

> Well, gentlemen, I propose to begin my eulogy of Socrates with a simile not because it is funny, but because it is true. What he reminds me of morer than anyone is one of those little sileni that you see in the statuaries' stalls, they are modeled with pipes or flutes in their hands, and when you open them down the middle there are little figures of the gods inside. And then again, he reminds me of Marsyas the Satyr.

Socrates is an "impudent satyr" as well as a "piper" but he needs no instrument to achieve the same effects. With Socrate's words we are "staggered and bewitched." And lastly, Alcibiades said: "Because, you know, he does not really care a row of pins about good looks — on the contrary, you cannot think how much he looks down on them — or money, or any of the honors that most people care about . . . he spends his whole life playing his game of irony, and laughing up his sleeve at all the world."[48] Cohen concluded from these remarks of Alcibiades that "with these words Plato has exactly pinpointed the Socratic power of the ugly."[49]

Cohen comprehended in beauty the ugly. The ugly is a way or a form that conceals the beautiful. The flute that Socrates plays, the good gods that appear from within him lead men to a beauty that is no longer momentary and arbitrary; it is the beauty of morality. The ugly is thus a fundamental element of our comprehension of the Idea of mankind. The question for Cohen is: Why is the ugly a more profound and more energetic power for the realization of a sense of humanity than the beautiful? "Now we can see that in the ugly slumbers the universal form of beauty, *das allgemeine Urbild der Schoenheit*."[50] The artist alone can reveal the fundamental relationship between the ugly and the beautiful. Cohen cited the example of Rembrandt. The apparently ugly are transformed by Rembrandt. Cohen remarks, "He makes them all worthy of love."[51] This is his healing power (*Heilkraft*). This relationship between ugliness and beauty was of great significance to Cohen. Here we comprehend the depths of his moral and aesthetic feelings: to see through ugliness into beauty, to develop the capacity to go beyond the immediate, the visible and audible, into that inner life where the little gods lie sleeping. There is pain and sadness when there are no more gods within. The deeper beauty must always be discovered, hidden as it is either by ugliness, "he had no beauty" or the appearance of beauty. Alcibiades' description evokes one of the deepest moments of Platonic thinking, a moment of invaluable meaning and force for every serious aesthetic discussion. Cohen felt deeply its moral implication. He repeated, "there is no true art without a truthful humanity,"[52] and continued with insight and pathos: "the purification of the moral condition has its validity in the treatment of folk types." Cohen admired Rembrandt's Jewish types, he felt deeply Rembrandt's openness to the Jewish people and noticed that the artist had his residence in the Jewish quarters. The feeling for humanity is not an abstraction, it is developed in intimate and prudent contact with life.

If aesthetics belongs to that relationship between the ugly and the beautiful, then the religious belongs to suffering and individuality. "The origin of the religious consciousness is not the love of God, but the love of the suffering person. The love of God comes forth with several meanings when God is recognized as the protector of the suffering."[53] Ultimately, nothing can be of significance if it does not contribute to a world in which the feeling for humanity is not augmented and deepened. Through our feeling for our fellow-man we draw God into the world. Our love draws him forth from his hiddenness, it brings him into correlation with the individual and with humanity. Although Cohen believed that in relationship to God the individual is discovered, the task of relationship is a universal one, dependent upon the activity of all men. The Idea of humanity is as fundamental to religion as it is for ethics and aesthetics. "Religious love will improve, ameliorate what the individual must suffer; aesthetic love in human suffering sees the glory of human kind, *Menschentum*."[54] Whatever the perspective, either that unique and demanding love relationship between man and God or man's needs to realize in his action the painful but glorious tasks that God has impsed upon him, man must bring ethical responsibility together with the beauty of its form and the feeling which it creates for the uniqueness of individuality. Knowing that God's love helps restore that wholeness that we call holy makes it possible to respond with courage and trust, to feel in this wholeness God's glory and beauty, to know that here lies the center of our task: to alleviate suffering and poverty, to make man again an end, and to deny any man or state the right to use man as a means.

After having structured a *Kulturphilosophie*, Cohen needed to find a place for religion. "The religious man is simply individual, *schlechthin Individuum*. This absolute individuality is given to him through his correlation with God. Through God man becomes an absolute individual."[55] This sense of individuality, this tenderness and sensitivity to its uniqueness forced Cohen to subject the aesthetic view to severe evaluation. It would seem that what emerged in Cohen's thought and feeling was not a willingness to set aside the ethical or the aesthetic, but to acknowledge to I-Thou correlation as the reality of religious man, who, aware of the structure of the Idea, of the command of the will and the creativity of the feeling, comprehends himself as individual in and through the God in whom hope and trust are fulfilled. Cohen was willing to say of aesthetic love that it is *"Phantasie"* the "sorcery of love."

Religious love is serious, aesthetic love only a mirroring, an abstraction, a "play with Ideas." This all may be true but what would religious love be without the aesthetic? Are we ever capable of separating these loves? Would the love for God that has now become puritanical in its puirty satisfy the endless levels of creativity that the aesthetic *eros* brings forth? In that *eros* so much of man's imagination is at work that we cannot but believe that it is another way for man to respond to his fellow-man, to humanity, to God. What was decisive for Cohen in this discussion was the fact that man in suffering, in the pain of finitude, finds comfort and relationship only with God. Man, without God, cannot discover this intimate I-Thou dialogue in any other spiritual relationship. *Kulturphilosophie* provides no place for man's loneliness and anxiety, for the nothingness that faces him in finitude. Art is man's love for form, the universality of the imagination.

The covenant between God and man is God's work of art, not man's. "God comes forth, he engenders himself in this covenant with man."[56] Cohen reached the conclusion that the thought of God bears within it the thought of man, and to think of man is impossible without relationship to God.[57] The religious reality is neither focused on God nor on man. In correlation we discover the meaning of the religious commitment. We also find the beauty that belongs to the manifestation of divinity. There is no correlation without beauty. The covenant, Cohen told us, is God's work of art. It is the universal expression of his glory, *Herrlichkeit,* his bond with every man and in whom every man is equal. In correlation the bond which God makes with man finds its realization. In it the intimacy of love and trust begin their painful and joyful odyssey. Man can only trust, have the courage of persistence, and love in spite of disillusionment and hardship. Religion is not the activity of the hero, but it is also not the venture of the fainthearted. To feel for the concerns of our fellowman, to be sensitive to inequality, hunger and pain, what Cohen refers to as *Mitleid* does not come forth in relgion. It is developed in morality and aesthetics and becomes the commitment of religion. God's covenant is beautiful because it projects the meaning of community to mankind. It is the community in which man finds responsibility through feeling and love. God, having formed a covenant with mankind, teaches man to form communities in which comprehension of mutuality reflects a correlation that we call beautiful. This community of mankind commands our imagination, stirs our hopes and shapes our sense of dependence and responsibility.

We comprehend Cohen's attempt to find that peculiar reality of religion when we know how deeply he loved lyric poetry. In a section of his *Aesthetics*, titled "The Humanity of Goethe's Lyrics," Cohen writes: "This love song is the document of humanity. This humanity is the new, free morality which is independent of the compelling force of forms of belief."[58] Speaking of Goethe's love songs Cohen reflected upon their freedom from dogmatic captivity and the true sense of humanity they embody. Humanity is true not through the abstract notion of love of neighbor, *Naechstenliebe,* but through the love of man, which art alone is able to strengthen and teach through its love for the nature of man. In the love of the love songs the nature of man is clearly brought forth. In its recognition and development true humanity is most clearly and effectively affirmed. Goethe's lyric has its supreme aesthetic value in this affirmation of humanity.... This love is pure because in it feeling is pure." Goethe, like Mozart and Rembrandt, was Cohen's spiritual "colleague." These men were his ever-present companions. We know a philosopher by the men and ideas he admires and lives with. In the Psalms, Cohen knew the beautiful lyric poetry of his beloved Bible. He quoted Psalm 51. "Turn away thy face from my sins and blot out my guilt. Create a pure heart in me, O God, and give me a new heart and steadfast spirit, do not drive me from thy presence or take thy holy spirit from me."[60] Closeness to God, trust and dependence upon Him, this experience was Cohen's throughout his life. He wrote philosophy with passion; he believed in it with devotion, he lived its consequences with courage and persistence. He expressed himself through forceful and commanding commitment to every genuine human experience. "Neither *Mitleid* nor longing, nor love, nor closeness are more than words. Through these words we only designate the problem that makes religion a peculiarity of consciousness, *Eigenart des Bewusstseins.*"[61] The question is the realization, the meaning, the reality of this *Eigenart.* The problem for us is its relationship to aesthetics, to that community of humanity in which Cohen believed, to his companionship with Mozart, Rembrandt, Goethe, in whom he found a communicating love for those Ideas and values which he believed philosophy needed to elaborate and communicate to all men. Cohen was a *Kulturphilosoph* but he knew that *Kulturphilosophie* in its universality was not enough without correlation, the Covenant, and above all, that distinct love and faith that he felt in the Psalms.

In the final chapter of *Religion of Reason,* Cohen remarked that "in the *Aesthetics of Pure Feeling,* I have tried to show that the feeling of being moved furnishes proof of the aesthetic consciousness. However, this view does not contradict our attempt at this time to claim the feeling of being moved for the religious consciousness in its virtuous way of peace.... This feeling is the love for the nature of man which, expressed in its pureness, shines forth in the countenance of man where it reflects the splendor of the pureness of being moved.... With the feeling of being moved, however, it is not the presence of man which compels me to have respect; rather a mere abstraction, which may be a story, an invention, brings a tear into my eyes.... Peace comes over me and animates me, even if I only fear of an invented action of goodness which a man allegedly achieved."[62] With these words, Cohen returned us to his love for Mozart and Goethe and Rembrandt. In the aesthetic feeling, Cohen discovered wholeness, *Das Heile,* not salvation, *das Heil,* the feeling for mankind that joins the individual to the universal, that gives him his moral health, *Salubriter,* or that feeling of wholeness that Cohen called peace. What enhances our feeling for our fellow-man, for the Idea of Humanity, for that correlation that brings us closer to God belongs to that cultivation of consciousness that relates logic to will and will to feeling, that wholeness which permits us to be aware of the needs of Papageno and the moral purpose of Tamino. Cohen was a member of that universal community where love and wisdom taught mankind the sicknesses of exaggerated individuality and hate. Is it surprising that Cohen heard in Mozart's music man's freedom and nature's redemption? Do we find it strange that Cohen's memorable contribution lies in his belief that religion is possible only when we love knowledge, feel the sublimity of the moral law, cultivate that feeling for human suffering and, above all, deny that true existence belongs exclusively to the present? The hope, trust and courage demanded by the future is the basis for that universality that is the beautiful form of true religious community. Where beauty cannot accompany belief in correlation there is no true religious community, no comprehension of that peace, *Shalom,* in which man again glimpses wholeness, that feeling of *Salubriter* that is goodness, beauty, and truth.

Philosophy has taken many directions in the twentieth century and philosophers must evaluate these directions. If we still have a fundamental commitment to reason, and to the belief of reason, then we must continue in the direction that Kant has set forth and which Cohen, Cassirer, Löwith, and Eric Weil have elaborated and developed. The belief in reason and universality is immutable if the Idea of Humanity remains constant. Universality and community are indelible Ideas for every thinker whose belief in rational critique is the presupposition of thinking, and whose acknowledgment of coherent discourse is an article of rational belief.

Conclusion

These essays were written from the conviction that reason is man's most precious gift and that his commitment to its ever increasing and demanding powers is binding. We are constantly attempting to grasp its encompassing reality, to read the cyphers of its manifestations and to follow the imagination in its never ending desire to read the divine script in the empirical existence in which we carry through our daily lives. Cohen's universalism was never able to show the fullness of its meaning because the philosopher fought battles that for us are no longer valid. The philosopher has no homeland other than the reason to which he had given his life. Cohen's struggle with his German heritage has little importance for us today. When he spoke of Judaism he found again the vehicle of humanism but even here his appreciation of Christianity, Islam, not to mention Hinduism and Buddhism, left much to be desired in appreciation and concern. Cohen remained a polemicist for his faith in a society where it was threatened with racism and Christian prejudice. It was in the universality of the ethical idealism of the prophets, in the union of ethics and aesthetics in Mozart that Cohen found the voices, the melodies, the words that spoke his universal ideas. Music through Mozart, like Plato's ideas, awakened in man compassion for suffering and ethical purpose; it gave him glimpses of unity and love.

The heritage of Cohen passed neither to Franz Rosenzweig, Martin Buber or Emmanuel Lévinas; it went to Ernst Cassirer and his philosophy of symbolic forms, and, even more, to Hugo Bergman's global perception of the transcendent unity of religions. Cohen gave us the task in both philosophy and religion which, I believe, is ours for the future: the creation of a communication of faith and reason in universal communication and interpretation. This would be the beginning of the realization of Cohen's *Idea of Humanity*. This requires the courage and loyalty to the encompassing powers of faith and truth in which we transcend empirical existence and struggle for the realization of the idea and the ideal. These essays continue those beginnings of universalism that are so rich in Platonic and Kantian idealism but are always conscious and sensitive to the immediacy of human problems and reveal a compassion for suffering and poverty in which we discover fellow-man.

Cohen's thought needed the decades of political and moral upheaval to find its way back to a world in search of loyalty to the ideas of freedom and truth. Philosophy has sought through the ages to set before the world the forms of reality, the *eidos,* which Plato taught us to be the essence of philosophy. We have tried to find the ways of participation, the *methexis,* to bring the ideas closer to us. We have neither succeeded nor failed. We have struggled for a form or idea of mankind, for friendship, for justice and we have never surrendered these vague terms because of vagueness. We have seen in them universal truths that make them necessary, demanding, challenging and necessarily vague. Plato said in the *Phaedrus* that in beholding them man sees "a beauty whose nature is marvelous indeed, the final goal of all previous efforts. This beauty is first of all eternal; it neither comes into being nor passes away, neither waxes nor wanes; next it is not beautiful in part and ugly in part . . . he [man] will see it as absolute, existing alone with itself, unique, eternal."

Cohen urged us to remain loyal to the eternity of ideas, to learn to be sensitive to their powers; to read our history as their revelation and the truth of our reason. He was the philosopher who, in teaching us Kant, taught us Plato's idealism. He put into our hands a sublime teaching and tradition. We continually learn it. We must escape the exclusivity and domination of empirical existence. We do this with the courage for the Idea, in loyalty to freedom and truth.

Notes

Preface: An Endeavor to Begin

1. *Philosophie der Vernunft und Religion der offenbarung in H. Cohen's Religionsphilosophie* (Heidelberg, 1968), p. 23. The shortened form of this essay was given in Marburg on June 21, 1968.
2. *Religion of Reason out of the Sources of Judaism*, p. 453.
3. Löwith, p. 9.
4. *Religion of Reason*, p. 36.
5. Ibid., p. 44.
6. Kant, *Critique of Practical Reason*, trans. L. W. Beck (Chicago: University of Chicago Press, 1950), IX: "Of the Wise Adaptation of Man's Cognitive Faculties to His Practical Vocation" (pp. 248-49).
7. *Kants Begründung der Ethik* (Berlin, 1910), p. 368. This is the most detailed and fundamental treatment of Kant's *Ethics*.
8. Ibid., p. 251.

Chapter 1
The Ecumenical Meaning of Cohen's *Religion of Reason*

1. *Religion of Reason out of the Sources of Judaism*, trans. S. Kaplan (New York, 1977), p. 453.
2. Ibid.
3. *Meaning in History* (Chicago, 1949), p. 17.
4. Ibid., p. 195.
5. Ibid., p. 194.
6. Ibid., pp. 197, 196.
7. *Religion of Reason*, p. 250.
8. Ibid., p. 200.
9. Ibid., p. 251.
10. *Meaning in History*, pp. 197-98.
11. *Religion of Reason*, p. 396.
12. Ibid.
13. Ibid., p. 398.
14. Ibid.
15. Ibid., p. 370.
16. Ibid., p. 420.
17. Ibid., p. 421.
18. Ibid.
19. Ibid., p. 424.
20. Ibid., p. 427.
21. *Begriff der Religion im System der Philosophie* (Giessen, 1915), p. 128.
22. *Religion of Reason*, p. 438.
23. Ibid., p. 440.
24. Ibid.
25. Ibid., p. 443.
26. Ibid., p. 460.
27. Introduction, p. xxxviii.

28. *Philosophische Lehrjahre* (Frankfurt am Main, 1977).
29. Ibid., p. 421.
30. Ibid.
31. *Ethik des reinen Willens* (Hildesheim, 1981), p. 411.

Chapter 2
Monotheism and History: The Heritage of Hermann Cohen

1. *Der Begriff der Religion im System der Philosophie* (Giessen, 1915). "Als dieser Schwerpunkt trägt Gott einzig das Sein, bedeutet und verbügt er allein das Sein. Der Natur und dem Mensch gegenüber ist er daher der Einzige" (p. 137).
2. Ibid., p. 136.
3. *Religion der Vernunft aus den Quellen des Judentums* (Frankfurt am Main, 1929), p. 185.
4. Ibid., p. 182.
5. Ibid., p. 183.
6. Ibid.
7. Ibid., p. 184.
8. Ibid.
9. Ibid., p. 183.
10. *Ethik des reinen Willens* (1907; Hildesheim, 1981), p. 629.
11. *Grundfragen der Philosophie: Geschichte, Whrheit, Wissenschaft* (Frankfurt am Main, 1965). In 1931 he published *Philosophie und Moral in der Kantischen Kritik* (1931; Tübingen, 1967); *Einsicht und Leidenschaft: Das Wesen des platonischen Denkens* (1939; 1963); *Freiheit und Weltverwaltung* (Freiburg, 1958); *Religiöse und profane Welterfahrung* (Frankfurt, 1973; posthumously published by Richard Schaeffler).
12. "Martin Heidegger und Franz Rosenzweig: Ein Nachtrag zu 'Sein und Zeit,'" in *Gesammelte Abhandlungen: Zur Kritik der geschichtlichen Existenz* (Stuttgart, 1960), p. 69 n. 2.
13. *Grundfragen*, p. 5. "Wir leben in einer Zeit totaler und freier Geschichtlichkeit." "Die Geschichtlichkeit des Lebens ist extrem geworden."
14. Ibid., p. 7. "Was er ist und sein muss, um ein Mensch zu sein, das muss er selbst bestimmen."
15. Ibid., p. 147.
16. *The Star of Redemption*, trans. W. W. Hallo (New York, 1971), p. 215.
17. *Confessions* X, 27, trans. R. S. Pine-Coffin (Penguin Books, 1961).
18. *The Star*, p. 259.
19. *Grundfragen*, p. 280.
20. Ibid. ". . . ein Kern von unüberwindlicher, wahrer, gemeinsamer Menschlichkeit."
21. *The Star*, p. 335.
22. *Grundfragen*, p. 281.
23. *The Star*, pp. 176-77.
24. *Religiöse und profane Welterfahrung*, pp. 92-93.
25. Ibid., p. 147.
26. *Philosophies of Judaism*, trans. D. W. Silverman (New York, 1973), p. 413.

27. *Ethik des reinen Willens*, p. 331.
28. *Philosophies of Judaism*, p. 440.
29. *An Essay on Man: An Introduction to a Philosophy of Human Culture* (New Haven, 1979), pp. 24-25.
30. Cassirer, "Judaism and the Modern Political Myths," in *Symbol, Myth, and Culture: Essays and Lectures* (New Haven, 1979), p. 241.
31. *Ethik des reinen Willens*, pp. 331-32.
32. *Logique de la philosophie*, 2nd ed. (Paris, 1974), p. 182. The category of God is discussed in Chapter 5.
33. Ibid., p. 183.
34. Ibid., p. 187.
35. Ibid., p. 188.
36. Ibid., p. 191.
37. *The Star*, p. 21.
38. "Problèmes kantiens," in *Archives de la Philosophie*, vol. 34, no. 2 (1971).
39. *Ethik des reinen Willens*, p. 331.
40. In *Savoir, faire, espérer: Les limites de las raison* (Brussels, 1976).
41. Ibid., p. 283.
42. *Faith and Reason: Modern Jewish Thought* (New York, 1976).
43. Ibid., p. 51.
44. *Religion der Vernunft*, p. 76.
45. *Republic* X, 617, trans. Paul Shorey, in *The Complete Dialogues of Plato* (Princeton, 1973).
46. *The Myth of the State* (New Haven, 1979), p. 296.
47. "Philosophy and Politics," in *Myth, Symbol, and Culture*, p. 230.

Chapter 3
Time and History: The Conflict between Hermann Cohen and Franz Rosenzweig

1. *The Philosophy of Symbolic Forms*, Vol. 2: *Mythical Thought* (New Haven, 1955), p. 120. *Religion der Vernunft aus dem Quellen des Judentums* (Frankfurt am Main, 1929), p. 291.
2. *The Star of Redemption*, trans. W. W. Hallo (New York, 1971), III, 1, 329.
3. *Le Christianisme "mis à nu"* (Paris, 1970), chap. V, "Hétéronomie et mauvaise infinitude," pp. 161-224. The chapter deals with both Hermann Cohen and Franz Rosenzweig.
4. Ibid., p. 200.
5. Ibid.
6. *Ethik des reinen Willens* (Hildesheim, 1981), p. 461.
7. *The Ages of the World*, trans. F. de Wolfe Bolman, Jr. (New York, 1967), p. 148.
8. For a discussion of this problem see Dieter Jähnig, *Schelling: Die Wahrheitsfunktion der Kunst* (Pfullingen, 1969), pp. 256-57.
9. Ibid., p. 256.
10. Ibid.
11. *Christianisme*, p. 202.

12. *Star* III, Gate, p. 420.
13. *Christianisme*, p. 203.
14. "Apologetic Thinking," in *The Jew: Essays from Martin Buber's Journal, "Der Jude," 1916-1923* (Philadelphia, 1980), p. 267.
15. Ibid., p. 272.
16. *The Ages of the World*, p. 204.
17. *The Star*, III, 411.
18. *Christianisme*, p. 204.
19. "The New Thinking," in *Franz Rosenzweig: His Life and Thought*, presented by N. N. Glatzer (Philadelphia, 1953), pp. 203, 204.
20. *The Star*, III, p. 290.
21. *Christianisme*, pp. 207-08.
22. *The Star*, III, p. 331.
23. *Christianisme*, p. 212.
24. *The Star*, III, pp. 341-42.
25. *Die Religion der Vernunft aus dem Quellen des Judentums* (Leipzig, 1919), pp. 307ff., 293ff. Quoted in *Meaning in History* (Chicago, 1949), pp. 17-18.
26. *Philosophy of Symbolic Forms*, II, p. 120.
27. *Ethik des reinen Willens*, p. 409.
28. Ibid., p. 410.
29. Ibid., p. 411.
30. Ibid., p. 406.
31. Ibid.
32. Ibid., p. 427.
33. Ibid.
34. *Religion of Reason our of the Sources of Judaism*, trans. Simon Kaplan (New York, 1972), p. 250.
35. *Werke*, Vol. II: *Antrittsvorlesung* (Munich, 1966), p. 19.
36. *Religion of Reason*, p. 453.
37. Ibid., p. 458.
38. Ibid., p. 249.
39. Ibid., p. 250.
40. Ibid., p. 233.

Chapter 4
The Conflict with Myth and Evil

1. *Ethik des reinen Willens*, Introduction by S. S. Schwarzschild (New York: Hildesheim, 1981).
2. Note 1, p. xxx.
3. *Problèmes kantiens* (Paris, 1970). "Ce n'est pas pour dévaluer l'homme, c'est pour lui donner sa chance d'humanisation que Kant parle du mal radical" (p. 173).
5. "Idea for a Universal History with a Cosmopolitan Purpose," in *Kant's Political Writings* (Cambridge University Press, 1970), 4th proposition, p. 44.
6. *Religion within the Limits of Reason Alone*, trans. T. M. Greene and H. H. Hudson (New York, 1960), II:51, note.
7. Ibid., p. 46.
8. Ibid., p. 30.

9. *Anthropology from a Pragmatic Point of View*, trans. M. J. Gregor (The Hague, 1944), p. 185.
10. *Religion*, p. 78.
11. "On the Failure of Attempted Philosophical Theodicies," in M. Despland, *Kant on History and Religion* (Montreal and London, 1973), p. 291.
12. Ibid., p. 292.
13. Ibid., p. 290.
14. Ibid., p. 294.
15. Ibid., p. 295.
16. Ibid., p. 296.
17. *Ethik*, p. 361.
18. Uriel Tal, *Christians and Jews in Germany: Religion, Politics and Ideology in the Second Reich, 1870-1914* (Ithaca: Cornell University Press, 1975), p. 282.
19. *Ethik*, p. 458.
20. Schelling wrote his *Philosophical Inquiries into the Nature of Human Freedom and matters connected therewith* in 1809. English trans. James Gutmann (Chicago, 1936).
21. Ibid., p. 84.
22. Ibid., p. 85.
23. Ibid., p. 90.
24. E. Fleishmann, *Le Christianisme "mis à nu"* (Paris, 1970), p. 165.
25. Ibid., p. 166.
26. *Critique of Judgment*, trans. J. C. Meredith (Oxford, 1969), #87.
27. Ibid.
28. Ibid.
29. "On the Failure of All Attempted Philosophical Theodicies," p. 292.
30. Kant, *Religion*, p. 77.
31. Ibid., p. 114.
32. Ibid., 121.
33. *Religion der Vernunft aus den Quellen Judentums* (Frankfurt am Main, 1929), p. 266.
34. *Der Begriff der Religion im System der Philosophie* (Giessen, 1915), p. 128.
35. King James Version.
36. *Der Begriff*, p. 129.
37. Ibid.
38. Ibid., pp. 129-30.
39. *Christianisme "mis à nu,"* p. 161.
40. E. Cassirer, *The Philosophy of Symbolic Forms*, Vol. 2 (New Haven, 1955), p. 4.; pages 3-12 are an excellent analysis of Schelling's thoughts on mythology.
41. Ibid., p. 5.
42. "The Polish Jew," in *The Jew: Essays from Martin Buber's Journal der Jude, 1916-1928*, selected and ed. A. A. Cohen (University of Alabama Press, 1980), p. 57.
43. Ibid., p. 59.
44. *Ethik*, p. 629.
45. *Myth of the State* (New Haven, 1979), p. 296.
46. Cited in G. A. Craig, *The Germans* (New York, 1982), p. 206.
47. Ibid.
48. *Ethik*, p. 629.

49. Ibid., p. 630.
50. Ibid., p. 632.
51. *Religion der Vernunft*, p. 23.
52. Ibid., p. 520.
53. Ibid., p. 522.
54. Ibid.,p. 523.
55. Ibid.
56. Ibid., p. 294.

Chapter 5
The Despair of Ressentiment and the Power of Compassion

1. Max Scheler. Now in *Vom Umsturz der Werte: Abhandlungen und Aufsaetze* (Bern: Francke Verlag, 1955).

2. Max Scheler, *Ressentiment*, trans. W. W. Holdheim (New York: Free Press of Glencoe, 1961), pp. 45-46.

3. Friedrich Nietzsche, *The Geneology of Morals*, in *The Basic Writings of Nietzsche*, trans. and ed. with commentary by W. Kaufmann (New York: Random House, 1968), p. 471.

4. Ibid.
5. Ibid.
6. See the three volume edition edited by Karl Schlechta.
7. Ibid., p. 470.
8. Ibid., p. 472.
9. Ibid.
10. Friedrich Nietzsche, *Daybreak: Thoughts on the Prejudices of Morality*, trans. J. Hollingdale (Cambridge: Cambridge University Press, 1982), p. 206.

11. Alain Besançon, *Les Origens intellectuelles du Leninisme* (Paris: Calmann Levy, 1978), p. 253.

12. Ibid., p. 15.
13. Ibid., 512.
14. Cited in K. D. Bracher, *The German Dictatorship: The Origin, Structure and Consequences of National Socialism* (Penguin University Books, 1973), p. 87.

15. Ibid., p. 88.
16. Friedrich Nietzsche, *Thus Spoke Zarathustra*, in *The Portable Nietzsche*, selected and trans. by W. Kaufmann (New York: Viking Press, 1968), p. 211.

17. Ibid.
18. Ibid.
19. Besançon, *Leninisme*, p. 296.
20. Ibid., p. 261.
21. Nietzsche, *Zarathustra*, "On the Tarantulas."
22. Besançon, *Leninisme*, pp. 298-99.
23. Fritz Kaufmann, "Karl Jaspers and a Philosophy of Communication," in *The Philosophy of Karl Jaspers* (La Salle, Ill.: Open Court, 1981), p. 274.

24. Hermann Cohen, *Religion of Reason*, trans. S. Kaplan (New York: Frederick Ungar, 1972), pp. 114-15.

25. Ibid., p. 137.
26. Ibid., pp. 140-41.

Chapter 6
The Abyss of Contradiction: Peace and Hatred

1. Hermann Cohen, *Religion of Reason out of the Sources of Judaism*, trans. with introduction by Simon Kaplan (New York: Frederick Ungar, 1972), pp. 448-49.
2. Ibid., p. 449.
3. Ibid., p. 451.
4. Ibid., p. 452.
5. Ibid.
6. Ibid.
7. Ibid.
8. Immanuel Kant, *Metaphysics of Morals*, Part II, *The Doctrine of Virtues*, trans. M. J. Gregor (New York: Harper Torchbooks, 1964), p. 131.
9. Immanuel Kant, *Anthropology from a Pragmatic Point of View*, trans. M. J. Gregor (The Hague: Martinus Nijhoff, 1974), p. 88. These remarks on the *sensus communis* and the *sensus privatus* are remarkable observations on the madness and hatred that accompany human isolation and the loss of community.
10. Cohen, *Religion of Reason*, p. 452.
11. Ibid., p. 453.
12. Ibid.
13. Ibid.
14. Ibid.
15. Ibid., pp. 453-54.
16. Ibid., p. 454.
17. Ibid.
18. Ibid.
19. Ibid.
20. Ibid., p. 457.
21. Ibid. p. 460.
22. Ibid., p. 461.
23. Ibid., p. 462.
24. Kant, *Metaphysics of Morals*, p. 157.
25. Ibid.

Chapter 7
The Opposition to Kantian Ethics

1. Cited in the article on Léon Brunschvicg in *Dictionaire des philosophes* (A-J), ed. Denis Huisman (Paris, 1984), p. 413.
2. Hermann Cohen, *Religion of Reason out of the Sources of Judaism* (1919), trans. S. Kaplan (New York: F. Ungar, 1972), p. 15.
3. Ibid.
4. Immanuel Kant, *The Metaphysics of Morals*, Part II, *The Doctrine of Virtue*, trans. with an introduction and note by M. J. Gregor (New York: Harper & Row), #24.
5. Hermann Cohen, *Religion of Reason*, pp. 14-15.
6. Ibid., p. 15.
7. Ibid., p. 16.

8. Ibid.
9. Ibid., pp. 18-19.
10. Kant, *Metaphysics of Morals*, #34.
11. Ibid.
12. Ibid.
13. Cohen, *Religion of Reason*, p. 19.
14. Ibid.
15. Kant, *Metaphysics*, #34.
16. Cohen, *Religion of Reason*, p. 19.
17. Kant, *Metaphysics of Morals*, #35.
18. Ibid., "Casuisitical Questions," #35.
19. Cohen, *Religion of Reason*, pp. 19-20.
20. Ibid., 134.
21. Ibid., p. 135.
22. Ibid., p. 93.
23. Kant, *Metaphysics of Morals*, #27.
24. Cohen, *Religion of Reason*, p. 136.
25. Ibid.
26. "Karl Jaspers and a Philosophy of Communication," in *The Philosophy of Karl Jaspers*, ed. P. A. Schlipp (La Salle, Ill., 1981), p. 274.
27. Nietzsche, *Daybreak* (Morgenroete) *Thoughts on the Prejudices of Morality*, trans. R. J. Hollingdale (Cambridge: Cambridge University of Press), II, #134.
28. Cohen, *Religion of Reason*, p. 137.
29. Ibid., p. 138.
30. Ibid., pp. 119-20.
31. Ibid., p. 140.
32. Ibid., p. 143.

Chapter 8
The Aesthetic Consciousness and the *Religion of Reason*

1. *Religion of Reason out of the Sources of Judaism*, trans. S. Kaplan (New York, 1972), p. 455.
2. *Ästhetik des reinen Gefühls* (Berlin, 1912), 1:236.
3. Ibid., p. 200.
4. Ibid.
5. Ibid., p. 210.
6. Ibid., p. 213.
7. Ibid., p. 217.
8. *Der Begriff der Religion im System des Philosophie* (Giessen, 1915), p. 96.
9. Ibid., p. 98.
10. *Religion of Reason*, p. 145.
11. *Ästhetik*, p. 188.
12. Ibid., p. 189.
13. *Der Begriff*, p. 98.
14. *Religion of Reason*, pp. 146-47.
15. Ibid., p. 147.

16. Ibid.
17. Ibid.
18. Ibid., pp. 147-48.
19. Ibid., p. 148.
20. *Äs*t*hetik*, p. 234: "Aber sie kann dies nur dadurch sein, dass sie die Idee der Menschlichkeit, die Idee der Würde des Menschen von des Ethik emfängt, und stets von neuem sich durch sie begrunden lässt."
21. Ibid., pp. 198-99.
22. *Religion of Reason*, p. 149.
23. Ibid., p. 150.
24. "History as a System," in *Philosophy and History: The Ernst Cassirer Festschrift*, ed. Klibansky and Paton (New York, 1963), p. 284.
25. *Religion of Reason*, p. 158.
26. "History as a System," p. 319.
27. *Ästhetik*, p. 230.
28. Ibid., 2:244.
29. *Ethik des reinen Willens* (Hildesheim, 1981), p. 16.
30. *Religion of Reason*, p. 419.
31. *Der Begriff*, pp. 98-99.
32. *Ästhetik*, 2:27.
33. *Religion of Reason*, p. 419.
34. Ibid., p. 418.
35. Ibid., pp. 57-58.
36. Ibid., p. 38.

Chapter 9
Hermann Cohen and W. A. Mozart

1. G. Wilandt, "Einleitung" Hermann Cohen *Werke*, vols. 8-9, *Aesthetik des reinen Gefuehls* (Hildesheim, 1982), pp. vii-xvi.

2. Hermann Cohen, "Mozarts Operntexte, Zur 150. Widderkehr seines Geburtstages" 1905, in Schriften zur *Philosophie und Zeitgeschichte*, Vol. I (Berlin, 1928), p. 491.

3. Ibid. Es ist die Leidenschaft der sinnlichen Liebe, aber in einer ganz anderen Energie und Selbstbewusstheit, asl bei Figaro; die Leidenschaft als Urkraft der Menschen, sie wird der Grund im Wesen Don Juans., p. 504.

4. Karl Löwith, *Philosophie der Vernunft in Religiion der Offenbarung*, in Cohen's *Religionsphilosphie*, vorgelegt am 14. Dezember 1968 (Heidelberg, 1968) 27. "Die Zauberfloete wird se zum Gipfel der Humanitaet, mit der Cohen die Ethik beschloss, die aber ihrerseits der Religion des einzigen Gottes bedarf, um als rreine Ethik bestehen zu koennen." 28.

5. Cohen, "Mozarts Operntexte." "Das sittliche Ideal, die Verbruederung der Menschen, des Friedens auf Erden, in der Wirklichkeit der Politik, um Leben der Menschen und der Voelker, das ist der Sinn der Zauberfloete." 514.

6. Wolfgang Amadeus Mozart, "The Magic Flute," Libretto, E. Schikaneder, English version, Ruth and Thomas Martin (New York and London: G. Schirmer, 1951), 2.

7. Ibid.
8. Ibid. "Doch fuehl ich's hier wie Feuerbrennen." 4.
9. Ibid., p. 5.
10. Ibid., p. 8.
11. Karl Löwith. "Die wirkliche Tragik traf Cohens Frau: sie wurde 1942 im Alter von 82 Jahren nach Theresienstadt deportiert," p. 30, fn. 59. Löwith points to Cohen's tragic error: the belief that a philosopher must have a homeland. "Der philosophische Irrtum Cohens bestand nicht in seinem lebenslangen Bestreben, sich als Deutscher. Juden zu wissen, sondern darin, dass er es fuer noetig hielt, Deutschland zur vaterlaendischen Heimat zu haben, ueberhaupt als Philosoph eine 'Heimat' zu haben, als ob die geschichtliche Mitwelt und Umwelt, in die man zufaellig hinein geboren wird, auch schon das Eine und Ganze der Welt waere, um die es der Philosophie als dem Denken des Einen und Ganzen geht." Löwith's exiles, in Japan and the United States, his physical relationships with Japanese, American thinkers gave him the possibility to be a global philosopher.
12. "The Magic Flute," p. 9.
13. Ibid.
14. Ibid., p. 11. "Ohne die Sympathie ist kein Glueck auf Erden."
15. Ibid., p. 12.
16. Ibid. . . . lehre sie die Macht der Goetter erkennen.
17. Mozarts Operntexte, p. 515.
18. "The Magic Flute," p. 14. "Ich bin so ein Naturmensch, der sich mit Schlaf, Speise und Trank begnuegt."
19. Ibid., p. 16. "Immer ohne Weibchen leben waere wahrlich Hoellenglut."
20. Ibid., p. 20.
21. Ibid., p. 21.
22. Ibid.
23. Ibid., p. 23. "Verloren ist der Feinde Mueh. Die Goetter selbst beschuetzen sie."
24. Ibid., p. 24.
25. Ibid., p. 25. "Es siegt die Staerke und kroenet zum Lohn Die Schoenheit und Weisheit mit ewiger Kron."
26. Mozarts Operntexte, p. 519.
27. *Aesthetic des Reinen Gefuehls*, "Vorrade," vol. I, VIII.
28. Ibid., p. 18.
29. Ibid.
30. Ibid., p. xi.
31. Ibid.
32. Ibid., p. xii.
33. Ibid.
34. Ibid.
35. Immanuel Kant, *Anthropology from a Pragmatic Point of View*, trans. Mary J. Gregor (The Hague: Martinus Nijhoff, 1974), #53.
36. Immanuel Kant, *Critique of Judgment*, trans. J. P. Meredith (Oxford, 1969), #20.
37. Kant, *Anthropology*, #53.
38. Ibid.
39. *Aesthetics*, xiii.

40. Ibid.
41. Ibid.
42. "Ueber das Eigentuemliche des deutschen Geistes," in *Schriften zur Philosophie und Zeitgeschichte,* p. 546. "Es ist fuer die Fortfuehrung der deutschen Philosophie eine Frage nicht nur der geistigen Gesundheit, sondern schlechthin die Lebensfrage des deutschen Geistes fuer seine Wahrhaftigkeit: ob Kant oder Hegel." From Cohen's perspective nothing is more incomprehensible that Hegel's remark in the Preface to the *Rechtsphilosophie:* "Das was ist zu begreifen, ist die Aufgabe der Philosophie, denn das, was ist, ist die Vernunft." "To comprehend what is, is the task of philosophy, because what is, is reason." (Trans. T. M. Knopf.) The task of philosophy is not what is but what should be, the future over the present.
43. *Aesthetics,* xiv.
44. *Critique of Judgment,* #29.
45. Der Begriff der Religion im System der Philosophie (Giessen, 1915), p. 86.
46. Ibid., p. 88.
47. Plato, *Symposuim,* trans. M. Joyce, in Plato, *The Collected Dialogues,* ed. F. Hamilton and N. Cairns (Princeton, 1973), p. 215b.
48. Ibid., p. 216c.
49. *Aesthetics,* vol. 9, pp. 385-86.
50. Ibid., p. 387.
51. Ibid.
52. Ibid., pp. 381-82.
53. *Die Religion,* p. 89.
54. Ibid., p. 91.
55. Ibid., p. 92.
56. Ibid., p. 96. "Gott entsteht, er erzeugt sich in diesem Bunde mit dem Menschen; sein Ursprung ist der Bund mit dem Menschen. Dieser Bund ist das Kunstwerk Gottes, aber nicht das Kunstwerk des Menschen."
57. For a detailed study of Cohen's religious philosophy, see William Kluback, *Hermann Cohen: The Challenge of a Religion of Reason,* Brown Judaic Studies (Chico, Calif.: Scholars Press, 1984).
58. Aesthetic des reinen Gefuehls, vol. 8, 41.
59. Ibid., pp. 42-45.
60. *The New English Bible* (New York: Cambridge: University Press, 1972).
61. *Der Begriff der Religion,* p. 107.
62. *Religion of Reason out of the Sources of Judaism* (1919), trans. S. Kaplan (New York, 1972), p. 455.

www.ingramcontent.com/pod-product-compliance
Lightning Source LLC
Chambersburg PA
CBHW031629160426
43196CB00006B/340